Maternal Threads

~ A Memoir ~

Frances Susanne Brown

First Edition: 2015 High Hill Press
Revised Edition: 2018 Frances S. Brown

Cover Design by Frances S. Brown

Dedication

I dedicate this book to the three gracious ladies who shaped me into the woman I am today:

My mother, my daughter, and Charlotte.

A New Breed

Somewhere wedged in between Prohibition and the Jazz era, in early 20th century America, an un-girdling of the Gibson girl birthed a new breed of bitch. The flapper.

I can't honestly remember the first time I heard the term. What I do know is when I set to researching, to find out what the flapper culture was all about, I had a definite purpose in mind.

Well, not exactly a purpose: more precisely, a particular person.

My exploration into the feminist movement, the turning point for women in the early 20th century, was an inspired quest to find out more about the woman I'd known as my Aunt Charlotte. Charlotte Steuer was born in Maspeth, Queens, New York, in 1905. She was, according to my mother, her older "half-sister." Charlotte raised Mom after their mother died, which happened in or around 1934.

Simple math tells me that Charlotte turned fifteen years old in

1920. She and her mother lived in an apartment in a small community in Queens that later completely disappeared from the map. Winfield was absorbed into the neighboring community of Maspeth by the end of the Second World War.

None of this, at this point in my story, really matters.

What matters is that my mother—Ruth Lillian Fisher—according to her birth certificate, was born in the same, now non-existent town of Winfield in 1922. Ruth was a mere child in the 1920s. Although she grew up in the same household with Charlotte, she ended up a completely different animal.

Charlotte Steuer, according to my retrospective analysis, and having known her quite well in her later years, fit the mold of the classic flapper.

Early 20th century American social history has never been my area of interest. I knew the feminine role had undergone a bit of a revolution, from the lofty aspirations of Amelia Earhart to the daring escapades of Clara Bow and Louise Brooks. But other than aerial aspirations and daring fashion expressions—bound-flat breasts, dropped waist dresses, snazzy looking hats set to the music of the lively new genre of music, Jazz—I didn't really know much about 1920s history at all. Except for what I learned from the book my Aunt Charlotte gave me when I turned thirteen.

Lilly Dache's Glamour Book was written by the French hat designer who made her fortune in New York City in that era. A woman obsessed with all things fashion, Ms. Dache built a business empire on a foundation of hats. In her memoir, Dache states she came to the United States from France in 1924. Immigration records say it was really 1919. In any case, it was exciting to think that Lilly was a contemporary of Charlotte: two young women in the big city of New York in the 20s, only a few years apart in age.

Lilly Dache's story is truly one of inspiration. She arrived with determination to make her career as a milliner. With only thirteen dollars in her purse, but plenty of spunk and a strong vision, she began as a lowly sales clerk in Macy's selling hats. Within a few years, she had begun building her fashion empire on Madison Avenue.

My Aunt Charlotte and Lilly Dache were among the women of the early twentieth century who embraced the flapper attitude.

What does flapper mean? Where did the word originate? There are a number of theories.

Joshua Zeitz, in his book *Flapper*, describes her thus:

"—the notorious character type who bobbed her hair, smoked cigarettes, drank gin, sported short skirts, and passed her evenings in steamy jazz clubs, where she danced in a shockingly immodest fashion with a revolving cast of male suitors." Ivan Evans, in his Brewer's Dictionary of Phrase and Fable, likens her to "a young bird flapping its wings while learning to fly."

The flapper redefined femininity. She was a rebel. She yearned for equality, and so claimed the right to do all the fun things men had been doing all along. To her, prohibition was a dare. She learned quickly that a wink and a wiggle could hook her to the arm of a beau who would get her through the door of any speakeasy. "George sent me" was the password, ushering her into a dark, smoky place of drink and dance.

Gone were the confining steel and lacings of her corset, and her yards of carefully coiffed hair. Flappers adopted a new mode of dress, rebelling against once- flaunted bosom and curve. They deliberately hid their feminine physiques beneath dresses that fell in a straight line from shoulder to hip. But hemlines rose, revealing some leg. And since flowing tresses had long signified femininity, it was among the first of the stigmas to disappear. The bob came into vogue, as flappers chopped their hair to the chin or shorter.

And then there were the hats. Gone were the wide- brimmed head dressings, elaborately decorated and dripping in ribbons and flowers.

The cloche was born, a head-hugging style with or without a small brim. The flapper pulled it down over her ears; so far down she had to tip up her chin to see where she was going. More than practical, it conveyed an attitude interpreted as intentionally rebellious.

This was the social climate of the era when Lilly Dache came to New York. This was the time and the place where my Aunt Charlotte grew up. My mother was nothing like her half-sister, though Charlotte was Mom's sole female influence from age twelve on.

My maternal heritage was, quite literally, a conundrum.

Revelation

My life-changing moment wasn't really very dramatic. The revelation didn't manifest at three a.m., alone on a bathroom floor in a pool of tears. I didn't awaken in a stranger's bed with a massive hangover, having not the slightest clue where I'd been the night before. In short, I didn't experience a mental breakdown. I didn't snap, though you might say my revelation did come about due to a snapping of sorts.

My eyes were opened in a more subtle way. I was fifty-two years old and had raised three reasonably normal children, a daughter and twin sons. I remained happily married to the same man who fathered them for over half my life. I'd finally found my career niche after working twenty-five years in the same field. My good health was probably less due to proper diet and sufficient exercise than lucky genetics. Most people would have said I'd "arrived." Perhaps I had. Just not all of me.

We were living in Massachusetts, which placed twenty-one years and thirteen hundred miles between my only daughter and me. But thanks to the modern conveniences of a cellular signal and hands-free devices, we commuted together every morning. We both rose and began our workdays early, in certain seasons before even the sun was awake.

"Hey, Mama. Good morning."

"Hey, baby. How you feeling?"

She was thirty-one by then, but no matter how old she got...

5

Susie, quite predictably, launched into her daily, spirited soliloquy denouncing the indecency, immorality, and insanity of working before nine o'clock in the morning; how she was running late again; how she stayed up way too late again; and how the guy driving the car in front of her was a complete asshole for stopping at a yellow light. Now, she would never get to work on time.

As her perpetually too-loud voice blasted into my head out of the hands-free earpiece, I passed a jogger bouncing along wrapped in neon green Spandex. I remarked, "Susie, I don't need to start my day with an aerobic workout. Talking to you is all the adrenalin I can handle." Then I smiled to her giggle, and we went on to the small-talk chatter that mothers and daughters oftentimes share.

My daughter was, and still is, my best friend, though I am sad to say I didn't share this kind of relationship with my own mother. Don't misunderstand; my mother was ideal in every classic definition of the role. But as I matured and met her on equal ground, Mom gradually evolved into a cardboard cutout, like one of those vivid-hued, but perfectly flat, paper dolls I played with as a child.

That's how I remembered her since up until the day she died, I knew very little about her family or childhood. Her closest living relative, whom I knew as Aunt Charlotte, was nothing like Mom. I'd met a few distant cousins, questionably linked, only once or twice. Mom's ancestry remained mystery, a taboo subject, one that changed her mood to anxious and sad if pressed to elaborate. As for maternal roots, I really didn't have any. Attempts to draw out my family tree to a semblance of balance repeatedly fizzled and died.

Although I'd remained stable all my life, at least in marriage and career, over the latter ten years I'd become somewhat of a wanderer. We raised the children in Florida, near their grandparents. But once the kids were grown and on their own, we bounced from Florida to Texas to North Carolina—all in a span of five years. As a laboratory technologist, I had the freedom to live and work almost anywhere I wanted. My husband, fifteen years my senior, had retired early. He loved to travel and have new adventures, and had, at least so far, followed me wherever my nomadic heart led.

Why had we moved around so much? We weren't intentional transients. I'd landed wonderful jobs. We'd rent for the first few months, but then purchased lovely homes in great communities, every time convinced we were there to stay. We made new friends, planted gardens, found new favorite restaurants, and lived like newlyweds, starting our lives over in a brand-new corner of the world. Yet, I remained unfulfilled. I was happy, but somehow, still searching. But for what? What more could a woman possibly want?

We'd built a custom home in the western North Carolina foothills, complete with mountain views and a hot tub on the elevated deck. I worked in a small, community hospital eight miles away. The shrubs we'd painstakingly planted along the foundation had barely taken root when I spotted the online posting for the job in New England.

I jokingly mentioned it to my husband. "It's in a lab at a school of veterinary medicine," I said. Up until then, I'd always worked on the human side of health care: hospitals, a private laboratory.

"Let's go," he said without hesitation. "You know me. As long as I'm with you, I'll be happy anywhere."

Ah, the anchor he has been to my life. Such chivalrous loyalty. No wonder I've held onto the same man for so long.

Springtime in New England was miraculous. I'd forgotten the exhilaration when, after a long, snowy winter I'd not endured since my childhood in New York state, bare branches turned green, seemingly overnight. Buds burst into leaf and bloomed as if nature simply crept through the countryside one night, opening each tree like a verdant umbrella.

On one of those morning commutes, Susie chattered into one side of my head as a line of ornamental trees I pass en route every day dazzled me. Bradford Pears, they stood four abreast in full blossom. White petals packed each erect oval so closely they shimmered like spring snow against the glow of the sunrise. I noticed sadly one of the trees had not weathered the winter well. The last ice storm was to blame. The branches of that delicate species didn't flex much before they snapped. Half of the tree's usual symmetry was gone, carved out as though a hungry giant had plundered through and taken a bite.

That lovely May morning in 2009, more than halfway through my life, I finally recognized what was missing.

I was half a tree.

I needed to complete the equation. I knew plenty about my father's side of the family, but little to nothing about my mom's. These days one would think it's easy, what with Ancestry.com and numerous other online resources. But I knew so little about Mom's family; I couldn't even get off the ground. Her maiden name was different from her half-sister's, and I didn't know what Charlotte's maiden name was anyway. And by then, they were both gone. There were some records—Mom's birth and baptismal certificates. My younger brother, Frank, and I uncovered them after our parents passed away, but he had custody of those documents.

Frank had done some digging into ancestry sites after our parents passed but was only successful on Daddy's side. He proudly supplied me with a paternal family tree printed out on dozens of sheets he'd carefully taped into a paper carpet big enough to cover my living room floor. I knew the names of my great- great-great grandparents who were born and lived in Venice and Naples, Italy.

On Mom's side, he'd been able to find virtually nothing. That didn't seem to bother him since Mom was, well . . . Mom. She was Dad's wife. She was our mother. Ruth Lillian Fisher had been virtually absorbed into Dad's family. Who she was before that, where the roots of her own family tree had germinated, didn't seem to matter once she married my father.

That was enough for my brother—all three of my brothers, actually. We'd all grown up in a loving, secure family environment with lots of extended gatherings. But those gatherings took place with my father's relatives. We spent every holiday and almost every Sunday at Grandma's house in Brooklyn, the only grandmother we had, with our aunts and uncles: my father's brother and sisters.

The only times I could remember spending at Aunt Charlotte's house, my father wasn't with us.

As a woman, there was a part of me missing. I needed to know more about my mother's heritage. Before I could understand myself, I needed to complete the puzzle. I needed to fill out the branches of my half- tree.

So where could I begin? The only place to go was back in time. Aunt Charlotte was Mom's only relative we ever spent appreciable time with. By then, when I realized I needed to know more, Charlotte had already been dead over thirty years. She was my only key. My memories of her, from when I was just a little girl, suddenly held new significance.

Since my husband and I were back in the Northeast, we only lived a few hours from the place where Aunt Charlotte lived and died. It was time to go back and pay memory a visit.

***

The house in Bloomingburg, New York was still there, but we almost drove right past the tiny cape. So many trees were gone. The house seemed abandoned, exposed, standing alone on that mountainside. The picture differed so much from the snapshot in my child's memory; a cozy cottage nestled within a thick pine forest. Forty years had revolutionized the landscape.

The once creaky plank-bottomed porch was wrapped in plain beige vinyl and glass. This was the place we went to stay for a day or two, sometimes longer. For my mother and my little brother and me, it was a refuge, the place we ran to when Daddy started drinking again.

One entire wall of the tiny living room was made of glass. It made the space feel much bigger than it was. Standing before that invisible wall, I used to imagine I was flying, floating weightless above the tops of the tall pines. On early misty mornings, before anyone else was awake, I would sit on the floor close enough to make my own fog-bursts on the glass. Cross-legged in my pink flowered pajamas, I sat on a cloud. I counted the needled pine tops that spiked a fluffy floor.

Although most of those trees were gone, one did remain, right on the corner where I remembered. It was towering and massive, but someone had pruned its lower branches. It seemed so tall to me when I was only eight or ten, but back then the pine was probably not very tall at all. Round and lush like a Christmas tree, its heavy wide branches used to bow low to the ground.

It had been the perfect hideaway for my brother and me. The spongy needled bed smelled spicy and left our fingers tacky with pine sap. We spent countless summer afternoons hidden there, the sun warming the scent until it almost crackled in the air.

Whenever Mom wasn't sure about what was going to happen next, she took us to the mountains.

"Come on, kids, Uncle Bill is here. Climb up into the van and sit down on the blanket." Uncle Bill's van was dirty and smelled bad, like a greasy, old filling station. To make room for us, he'd crowded his jumbled supply of blackened tools into one rear corner. "Don't touch Uncle Bill's stuff. If you're good, maybe Aunt Charlotte will let you pet her new puppies!"

Mom's smile was bright, but her eyes couldn't lie. I guess I detected the quiver in her voice even though I was such a little kid. I knew something wasn't right. Why wasn't Daddy going with us? Why wasn't Daddy driving us, in our car?

Aunt Charlotte's poodle puppies were magic. She used to be a big-time breeder of fancy show poodles, but that was when she was younger and lived in Greenwich Village. Now she only raised a litter or two a year. Three or four pups, sometimes five in a litter, their pudgy bodies were wrapped in tightly curled fluff so much softer than any stuffed toy. Some were shiny blue-black, some the color of Hershey bars, others a delicate peach that reminded me of Mom's cobbler. But all the pups smelled the same, like damp newspaper. Wet little noses and tongues greeted us with an enthusiasm that told us we'd be forever friends. But Aunt Charlotte never let us cuddle with them too long. They were her special babies. She hoarded them more diligently than their own birth mother did.

The house was overrun with poodles. Some of the dogs were old and had lived there since they were born. Robbie was the oldest.

"You have to be careful around Robbie," Aunt Charlotte warned us in shrill tones every time we walked through the door and again several times after that. "He's old, and he's blind. He wouldn't want to hurt you, but he might snap if he gets frightened."

Robbie had patches of pink skin showing through a curly gray coat that looked like a balding old man's head. His skin felt funny, like a balloon filled with warm water. Robbie's eyeballs had a shiny white sheen over them, and he had two crooked, yellow fangs on his lower jaw that stuck out at weird angles. He always smelled bad, like a dirty diaper.

Aunt Charlotte loved her "babies," as she called them, almost as much as she loved her *stories*.

For a long time, right after lunch, we weren't allowed to play in the house unless we were very quiet, because *the stories* came on the TV. That's when my brother and I would go outside to play under the pine tree, or on the porch if it was raining. In wintertime, we built igloos, squinting in the brightness reflecting off the snow.

Mom called Aunt Charlotte a *glamour girl*. Sometimes she and my mother talked about the old days, back when Aunt Charlotte worked in a fancy office in Greenwich Village and wore all the latest styles. It was hard for me to imagine her like that, since Aunt Charlotte was old even when I was a little girl. She had a bulbous body and spindly legs. Her auburn hair was frizzy but never gray. I never saw her without her bright red lipstick.

She took good care of what she called *her complexion* with Pond's Cold Cream. Every night, before we climbed the stairs to the loft, she disappeared for a little while, and then reappeared in the doorway looking like a silly ghost. On her head, she wore a satin cap with ruffled lace edges. Her whole face was smeared thick with shiny, white goo that kept us from kissing her on the cheek when we said good night. Her lips stood out like a clown's, still stained bright red.

"Don't you laugh at me!" she shrieked. "If you use Pond's Cold Cream every night, your skin will be as soft and pretty as mine is when you're an old lady like me. You, my dear," she pointed at me, "should start doing that right now."

I still do.

On her bed were special satin pillowcases, so she wouldn't muss her hair. She had lots of them and washed them every day.

I remember dinnertimes, five chairs wedged at odd angles around a table meant for two. But dinner came right before bedtime. At Aunt Charlotte's house, my brother and I dreaded the end of day. We knew that when the darkness came we had to climb the narrow stairs to the attic loft.

The bare light bulb at the top of the stairs hung over a huge wooden cabinet that smelled just like the sheets: a little musty, a little like Downy, and a little like mothballs. She and Mom tucked us into twin beds that fit perfectly under a sloping roofline where we knew that sleep would come slowly, as the strangeness and the loneliness settled down over the tops of the well-worn quilts. There was no nightlight.

It was my job to fill the silence after the adults left us there, since I was the elder, though only barely. I chattered on about nothing, telling stories and ignoring the thick quiver in my brother's sleepy comments until finally, he fell asleep. Then I'd realize, from the sound of his slow, rhythmic breathing, that I was truly alone. That's when the thickness crowded my own throat as I fought back tears. But Aunt Charlotte always left the hall light on. The bulb hung from a porcelain fixture with a short, beaded chain. Its brightness glared relentlessly in through the doorway.

I could have pulled the soft, threadbare sheets up over my head, and the thickness of the blankets would have blocked the light. That's what my brother did. Or sometimes he rolled to face the wall, curling into that low and narrow place where the roofline came down to meet the mattress. I tried that, too, but it only felt more strange. Instead I would lie on my back, arms crossed under my head, facing that bulb, defying it through scrunched-shut lids.

With my eyes closed, I could imagine I was home, where the hall light outside my bedroom doorway burned until sleep overtook me. I had a good imagination. On those lonely nights at Aunt Charlotte's, I could make it take me home again.

Before sleep rescued, sounds bounced up the stairs, echoing in the hallway. I heard my mom and aunt's voices, but the tones were so different than during the daylight hours. I tried to understand the words, but for the most part, their conversations bled with pain too raw for me to even want to understand. Sometimes I heard my mother's sobs.

The daytimes weren't so hard. Aunt Charlotte always tried to make everything okay. I wondered about that sometimes, since I didn't completely understand what the problems were at home, so I couldn't see Aunt Charlotte was at all to blame. Her attention, though, sometimes overdone to outright coddling, was always welcome comfort.

"Let's bake something this afternoon . . . something gooky." That was her word for desserts, anything sugary and decadent. She hated to cook real food. Her favorite things were desserts and cocktails. One of her special recipes was for applesauce cake.

She taught me how to make it from scratch, starting with shiny, green apples. Aunt Charlotte peeled them slowly with a worn paring knife. It was my job to chop the crisp flesh into small pieces. We boiled them with cinnamon, in a huge, gleaming pot of steaming water until the whole house smelled like Christmas.

Then Aunt Charlotte set me to the real work. She had a huge silver colander that seemed big enough to sift the pain and loneliness out of the whole world. With a well-worn wooden spoon, I pushed the amber chunks through a star pattern of holes, filling a glass bowl that was green on the outside and milky white inside. Then we mixed the batter.

That first time she handed me the egg carton, I froze, wide-eyed.

"I've never broken an egg before. Not on purpose, anyway."

"You haven't?" Aunt Charlotte's thinly penciled eyebrows rose, and I instantly felt ashamed. "That's okay," she said quickly. "I'll show you how. I'll show you the right way."

My aunt lifted one of the eggs out of the cardboard carton. It was much bigger than the eggs we had at home, so white against her cherry red fingernails. So pure and perfect, it almost seemed a shame to ruin it.

"Now, you don't want to hurt the egg," she said. "You just want to open it up...so you tap it on the edge, like this." When Aunt Charlotte rapped the egg on the edge of the bowl, I blinked. Her hands moved too fast, but her brightly painted fingertips seemed to know what to do. The egg magically vanished from inside the shell and reappeared glistening in the bottom of the bowl.

"Now you try. Here, hold the egg like this. You just want to wake it up! Go ahead, don't be afraid...Good! Now, put both of your thumbs into the crack, right here. Just open up the shell and let it out."

My first try wasn't perfect. A fragment of bony shell floated atop the gelatinous mass that plopped too soon into the Pyrex bowl. Before tears sprung, a teaspoon appeared out of nowhere, or perhaps from the flowered china saucer under the cup of tea that always lived on the round table in front of Aunt Charlotte's place. The speck disappeared as though it had never intruded.

Waiting for the cake to cool took forever. She placed it on a blackened metal rack in the middle of the table, in the formal dining room, a room always blocked with a gate to keep the poodles out. The table never got used except to cool the cake and to hold the mountain of magazines and mail stacked all the way to its edges. She would shoo us away from the gate again and again until the old bell timer on the back of the stove chimed.

"Okay now, who wants the first piece? You know the first one is never shaped right," she purred through a conspiratorial smile. "But it tastes yummy just the same."

It didn't matter that the edges weren't perfect, or that it was too close to suppertime for snacks. None of that ever mattered when we were at Aunt Charlotte's house.

As much as we missed home and missed Daddy, we were still sad when it was time to leave. Sad because there would be no more afternoons of Mom and Aunt Charlotte talking about the old days while we peeled the apples for the cake. Sad because I couldn't whisper secrets with my brother in our piney hideout or giggle at Aunt Charlotte's silly, bedtime face. Sad because there would be no more excited strangeness.

When we stayed in the mountains, Mom always seemed to feel better. She called my aunt "Sis," and told us again and again how Charlotte had been like a mother to her, even though she was only her "half- sister."

"What does that mean, Mommy?"

"We had different fathers," she explained.

Charlotte was seventeen when my mother was born.

***

15

"Are you okay?" my husband asked.

We were sitting in his truck, parked on the shoulder of the road across the street from the house on the side of the hill. I had no idea how long we'd been there. I was surprised to see how high the sun had crept above the line of pines in the distance. It was late summer, and the cab was heating up fast. I noticed Clark had opened his window. How patient he could be. I forced my vision outward again, back to the present and into his concerned gaze. Blinking, I nodded.

"She was so very different from my mother," I said. Then, with a chuckle, I added, "You know, I think about her so often these days. The older Susie gets, the more she reminds me of Charlotte."

My husband lifted one eyebrow and cocked his head as he reached to turn the key. "Susie has a streak of independence, that's for sure. One I doubt she inherited from either you *or* your mother." He revved the engine and eased the truck onto the pavement, then turned to study me. "I never met your aunt. What was she like?"

I turned away toward the window, trying to hide the smirk I couldn't suppress.

"According to my father," I said quietly, "Aunt Charlotte was a floozy."

Sheltered

They say that one of the symptoms of Alzheimer's is that memories of the distant past come more easily than those of yesterday. On my quest to understand my maternal roots, at times I almost wished for an early onset of the dreaded disease to help me remember my childhood. But a simpler cure had been visiting Aunt Charlotte's old home; the trip acted like nasal spray for my brain. I found snippets of my early childhood flooding back. Spontaneously.

The memories surfaced while I was drifting off to sleep at night or lying awake in the throes of a hot flash at three a.m. (damn menopause!). The backs of my eyelids acted as a movie screen. I watched scenes recorded somewhere in a part of my brain, many I'd not been able to access since adulthood bound my consciousness within a tangled net of responsibility, and under the pandemonium of day-to-day life.

***

"Mommy, how come my friend Loraine has two grandmas and grandpas…and I have only one grandma? And no grandpas at all?"

I was six years old. It was another rainy Saturday afternoon. It didn't seem fair, but ever since I'd started school, it always seemed to rain on Saturdays. I didn't know where my little brother was; but since he wasn't bothering me, I didn't care. Daddy was asleep in front of the news on TV, and Mom was in her usual spot at the kitchen table. Legs crossed at the knee, her cigarette burned in an ashtray. A strand of bright yarn wove through her fingers, linking her to a patterned tote bag that sat on the scuffed linoleum floor.

We lived out in the country, without many neighbors, and none close by. My sole playmate, up until I'd started school, was my younger brother. He was more of an obligation than a friend. There were only two houses on Daly Lane besides ours. One was always empty, and the other one belonged to the weird, old Wanamakers.

Mrs. Wanamaker was scary. A small woman with fuzzy brown hair, she was quiet and jumpy, like a bird. She clutched her worn-thin, blue sweater tight across her chest, even in the middle of summer. And her eyes were very strange. Shiny and dark, they reminded me of the plastic ones on my stuffed animals. But unlike my toys' eyes, hers moved.

In contrast, I thought Mr. Wanamaker would have made a great grandpa. True, he was old and weird. But in truth, I had no grandpas. So how was I to judge? To my mind, he fit the stereotype, at least physically. He had a long, gray beard and wore round, wire-rimmed glasses. He didn't have any grandchildren of his own. Mr. Wanamaker was always nice to my brother and me, taking us into his garage to show off his shiny, dark green, antique car with a black top made of cloth.

My mother was wearing the same strange look as Mrs. Wanamaker after I asked about my lack of grandparents. She sat at the table, her gaze intent on her work and magnified behind her readers, fingers fluttering a shiny, metal hook around the multicolored, orange and yellow, yarn she was busying into an afghan.

"How come, Mommy? How come I have no grandpas?"

"Well," she began, "you know that Grandma is Daddy's mother. Daddy's father—your grandpa—died just after your father and me got married."

I paused, trying to understand. I knew Grandma, and she was the only one I had. She was Daddy's Mom. She lived with Aunt Sue and Aunt Madeleine and Uncle Paul—all together in one house, in the busy, dirty, noisy New York City. I had another aunt and uncle, too— Aunt Charlotte, who lived up in the mountains, with Uncle Bill and all those poodles. Her house was dirty and noisy, too, but on the inside. What I really didn't understand was how those people were all related—to each other or to us. It was too hard to think about.

My wandering six-year-old thoughts doubled back to the original question.

"What about your mommy and daddy, Ma?"

There was another long silence. My mother never looked up from her crocheting. Then she answered very quietly.

"Grandma died when I was twelve years old." "How did she die? Was she old?"

"She wasn't very old at all, but she wasn't well. She had a rheumatic heart."

"What's that?"

She sighed then, her fingers pausing as she looked up over her glasses. Staring past me, she looked so sad.

"Sometimes when I came home from school," she said, "I'd find her on the couch, so weak she couldn't get up. Her heart wasn't very strong. She sent me down to the corner store. The druggist would give me some medicine for her."

"Would she feel better then?"

"Sometimes," my mother answered, "but sometimes she didn't. Then Aunt Charlotte had to cook dinner."

I remember feeling sorry for my mother. For me, there was such comfort in knowing that when I came home from school, Mom would always be there. I knew she'd be sitting in her chair at the kitchen table with her latest needlework project, the smell of supper filling the house. Sometimes there was banana bread baking in the oven. Sometimes she'd be standing at the stove stirring a pot of homemade chicken soup. Sometimes it was chocolate pudding.

"That would be scary," I said. I didn't have an older sister. I wondered, if not for Mom, who would cook dinner?

"It was very scary. But what was even scarier was after she died because we were poor. We couldn't afford a funeral. They laid her out in our living room. My mother's body, in her coffin, right there in our living room. Three whole days passed before they buried her."

I felt a chill wash over me, like when I jumped into the still-icy pool at Loraine's house on the first day of summer.

"Weren't you afraid?"

My mother paused, seeming reluctant to answer me now.

"A little. But she was my mother, and I knew she would never hurt me. It was just hurt so much to see her lying there, her skin as white as the satin lining of the casket. She was so still. I couldn't understand why she wouldn't open her eyes. I didn't want to believe she would never move or talk to me or tuck me into bed ever again."

I didn't say anything for a long time.

"Is she buried in the graveyard near my school?" I'd never been in a graveyard, but I had seen headstones from the window of my first-grade classroom, across the road and enclosed by a black iron fence.

Mom had gone back to her crocheting and was quiet for a long time. I thought maybe she was counting her stitches. Finally, she said, "No, we lived in Queens when she died. We were very poor. I don't know where she is buried."

The crochet needle flashed faster and faster in and out of the loops of bright yarn.

"What happened to Grandpa? Your daddy . . . "

The needle stopped. My mother set the bright patch of yarn down on the table, carefully arranging the hook on top. She didn't say anything for another long time. Staring at her hands, she started rubbing them together, one over the other very slowly.

It was the same thing she did every time she and my father argued.

I waited a few minutes, but when Mom didn't answer, I thought maybe she'd forgotten what I'd asked.

"What happened to your daddy, Mommy?"

The way her voice was then, I thought maybe I'd made her mad at me.

"My father was a sailor, a fisherman," she said. "He died when I was a baby. I never knew him."

***

A shortage of grandparents was only one way in which I discovered I differed from some of my new friends at Our Lady of Mt. Carmel private elementary school. Those first few, traumatic months of first grade highlighted my lack of social skills. I'd never had many friends even close to my own age. We lived so far out of town, and my parents didn't socialize with many people who had children. In truth, they didn't socialize with many people at all. I quickly discovered just how awkwardly shy I really was.

Fortunately, on that fateful day when I joined twenty-two other kids whose parents wanted them raised "good Catholic boys and girls," I met Loraine Dassori. I'd like to thank fate, but it truly was a matter of the pre-determined, alphabetic seating chart—and my short stature. Since *Da* comes before *De*, I landed behind Loraine.

I couldn't even see the blackboard around Loraine's voluminous masses of dark, curly hair. The nuns quickly rearranged us according to height. Loraine ended up in the desk right next to mine.

Loraine and I had a number of commonalities. Her father was Italian, like mine, but neither of our mothers were. We'd already been drilled on the rules of being good girls, like not saying swear words, always saying "please" and "thank you," and never forgetting to bow our heads whenever we passed the altar in church.

We wore respectable clothes. No tee-shirts with printed messages or pictures and jeans that weren't too tight. We wouldn't dream of wearing makeup. Loraine and I sat together at every Christmas Eve Midnight Mass. Her father worked while her mom stayed at home, just like mine.

Like me, Loraine's contact with kids her own age had been limited. Her only sibling, Sharon, had been her assigned playmate up until that first day of school. I didn't have a sister, and the only one of my three brothers who wasn't too old to consider me a fat, little pain in the butt was the youngest, Frankie, who, to me, was a skinny, little pain in the butt—with buck teeth. Loraine looked at her sister in much the same way; though for Sharon, it was her eyeglasses that seemed too big for her face.

Loraine and I were both equally sheltered, although I was much shyer than her. I guess that's why I was immediately drawn to her when she smiled at me on the playground that first day of school. She was the first to say hello. It wasn't long before I willingly handed her the role of leader in our friendship, along with the extra slices of chocolate cake that my mother carefully wrapped with Saran Wrap especially for her, tucked into my lunch box. Or banana bread. Or sometimes a slab of that aromatic applesauce cake I'd brought home from my Aunt Charlotte's house.

Those were the years before Sesame Street and My Baby Can

Read. Kindergarten was also a relatively new concept and not required. Both Loraine and I entered the first grade straight from home. Neither one of us could read. So, in those early days, the first time we left the cafeteria by ourselves to use the bathroom was incredibly terrifying, but also exhilarating. I felt grown-up and independent—as long as I had Loraine with me. And the sensible, grown-up thing to do was to go pee before we stood in that long line to buy the carton of milk to go with the boxed or bagged lunch we'd brought from home.

The school had two bathrooms, side-by-side, halfway down the hallway. Bright pastel tiles formed a shiny border around the outside of each entrance, cleverly designed with little L-shaped foyers, so that doors weren't necessary. Beside each entryway was a plaque with letters that looked familiar, but refused to reveal their secret meaning to us, the two little girls who couldn't read. I'd only just begun to scratch letters of the alphabet in pencil between the wide, dotted lines of my notebook. Although I couldn't read the words on either sign, I wasn't really sure if they were all that important anyway. Neither one of us could remember which doorway Sister Mary Joseph had pointed to the day before.

I turned to Loraine. "Can you read?"

"No," she replied in a small voice. "Can you?" I shook my head.

"I wonder—does it matter which one we use?"

We glanced up and down the hallway, looking for a kindly face in a familiar black-and-white habit to help solve our dilemma. But the hall was empty and quiet since all the kids had rushed to the lunchroom to jostle for position in the line, herded by every available nun in the place.

"I dunno if it matters or not," Loraine said. We stood there in silence for a minute, waiting for some miracle to guide us. Then Loraine had an idea. "What's your favorite color?" she asked. I answered right away.

"Blue! It's my mom's favorite color, too."

We did notice the funny looking sinks along the wall in the bathroom with the blue sign, but there were two enclosed toilets, and it was empty. Loraine latched herself behind one stall door, I the other.

Before we were through, we heard footsteps, and the sound of water running. We didn't hear the voices until we'd flushed and opened the stall doors. In horror, we discovered two boys facing the funny sinks on the wall. They were older, probably from the sixth grade. Their shocked faces in the mirror turned quickly to mocking grins. Laughter bounced off the tiled walls and grew louder, louder even than the pounding of my heart, as I scurried out the door behind Loraine.

We didn't even stop to wash our hands.

Everyone in Our Lady of Mount Carmel wore uniforms: the girls in blue-green plaid pinafores and the boys in navy blue trousers with starched white shirts. We all had to wear the same stupid, plaid bow tie that I never could manage to clip on straight without Mom's help. Everyone not only had to wear the same clothes, but there were even rules about how the clothes were cared for.

A boy would get sent to the office for coming to school with a wrinkled shirt or a girl for having her skirt hemmed too short. The nuns actually used a ruler to measure the distance between the top of our kneecaps and the hem of our skirt. If there were more than two inches between, the principal called our parents and sent us home to correct this shameful condition.

Of course, this didn't stop some of the girls; because even after the hem of their skirts had been lowered to the acceptable level, they rolled up the waistband and tucked it behind the pinafore front. Mostly the sixth-grade girls dared, exposing just a little more of their pale, lightly fuzzed thighs to the boys on the playground who played stickball in the sand near the swings. Most of the boys didn't ever seem to notice. The girls were always careful to pull their skirts down to the acceptable level when recess was over. And there was a hat, at least for the girls.

Women in those days were not permitted to attend Catholic services without their heads covered. Our parish priest often said Mass in the school's tiny gymnasium (there was an obligatory feast day every week, it seemed). Since Mass was held during the school day, of course, we were wearing our uniforms.

Although our hats weren't required for every day, heaven forbid if a girl forgot to bring hers on a feast day. The nuns always had plenty of spare white hankies to mark the negligent. A bobby- pinned hankie not only pleased God, it also marked the offending student as effectively as a scarlet "A."

Those were also the days before Physical Education became a mandatory part of our educational system. We had "gym," as they called it, but our teachers were nuns and would have looked pretty funny trying to dunk a basketball wearing a long, flowing habit. Our gym teacher wasn't a nun. Miss Ruple had short-cropped hair and walked like a boy.

I'd never been much for sports and wasn't particularly coordinated to begin with, since I was still wearing orthopedic shoes for my crooked ankle. I guess that's why Miss Ruple never called me off the sidelines during the soccer or basketball games. We didn't even have to change out of our uniforms but were instructed to slip on our shorts underneath our skirts. None of this presented too much of a problem for me; I was hardly coordinated enough to work up a sweat.

Since we all dressed the same, nobody really noticed who was fat and who was not. My mother baked a lot, and at home we had a huge snack drawer perpetually stocked. I occupied many solitary hours after school lying on my bed with a book, accompanied by a plate heaped with brownies, a couple of Twinkies, or a mound of potato chips. In our mostly Italian family, a fat child was a visual statement of health and prosperity. My parents never limited my snacking and

25

encouraged second helpings at mealtimes since Daddy hated leftovers. Besides, it was a sin to waste good food.

And so, it was a real shock to me when this carefully monitored world of Catholic school at Mount Carmel came to an end. Sixth grade was the highest. The next step was the Goshen Christian School in a town about twenty miles away. Bus service didn't extend to where Loraine or I lived. I remember a family pow-wow taking place in our kitchen one Saturday evening that spring of 1969, when Loraine's parents and mine sat over steaming cups of espresso with knitted brows and serious voices.

The adults all settled around the white Formica table, and after a brief sprinkling of small talk, they all got quiet. Then my father began, "So, Artie, have you decided what you and Jeanette are going to do about the kids' school for the fall?" There were four of us "kids." Loraine and her younger sister Sharon, and myself and my younger brother Frankie.

Jeanette was the one who responded. "Well, we've been talking about this for a few weeks now, and we just don't like the idea of sending them to Goshen Christian." "I agree," my mother said. "It's too far to bus them, and I certainly couldn't drive them there." My mother had only just learned to drive a few years before. Loraine's mom could drive, but their family owned only one car. And then there was the cost. Tuition at Goshen Christian was much higher than at Our Lady of Mount Carmel.

"I just can't see as how we can afford it, not with two of them going," my father said. "Business has been pretty lean lately."

"We're in the same boat. Artie's not had a new building contract yet this month," Jeanette said. "But if we move them into public school, we're moving both Loraine and her sister. I don't think it's a good idea to separate them."

"Well there's that other issue as well, Frank." Artie finally found his voice, a gruff but surprisingly high-pitched one for the face it came out of. Loraine's dad was from Sicily, short and broad with a face like a bulldog, wearing the nose of an ex-prize-fighter even though he'd never thrown a punch—at least for money—in his life.

Loraine's mother cleared her throat, shifting in her seat and dropping her gaze so intently on her cup of coffee I thought there might be a bug floating in it. My mother responded with a quiet "mmm" but didn't say anything more.

My dad leaned forward towards Loraine's father, his expression tense as he asked quietly, "Who did you hear that story from, Artie?"

"It's no story, Frank—I heard it from the horse's mouth. One of my subcontractor's kids came back from senior trip that way. I thought an overnight trip was a stupid thing to do anyway. A Christian high school!" He shook his bald head slowly from side to side in a way that reminded me of an elephant swinging his trunk.

"What did they do about her, Artie?" my father asked.

"They shipped her off to her grandmother in Ohio. They didn't want everybody around here knowing about it. Plus, she's got a younger sister they were worried about."

There was a long silence in our kitchen. "It's a tough thing," Jeanette finally said.

My mother remained silent. Staring down at her hands, they were folded tight on the table in front of her as though intent in prayer. Her eyebrows were raised, but she didn't say anything at all.

My mother's reaction that night didn't mean anything to me at the time. I guess I just assumed the "situation" they were discussing was embarrassing to her. She was the perpetual lady, so prim and proper. I never heard her say the word "sex." I learned about menstruation from the nuns at school, just a few months before this family meeting in my last year of Catholic School. All the girls in my sixth-grade class were herded into the private conference room off Mother Superior's office.

They showed us a film, and while all my classmates whispered and giggled around me, I sat wide-eyed with my jaw dropped. I'm embarrassed to admit it now, but I was twelve years old before I learned anything about my own body, human reproduction, or that very bad word, "sex." When I got home that night and tried to tell my mother about the film I'd seen, she put a finger to her lips and dragged me into the bathroom, closing the door and locking it behind us.

"I guess I should have told you about all this by now, but I just couldn't talk about it," she whispered. She seemed sad, embarrassed. "I'm sorry you had to find out about it this way."

Mom made the whole reproductive process sound like a terminal illness, a curse that we, as women, should be ashamed of. Looking back, I wish now I'd thought to ask my Aunt Charlotte about it. I think talking to her, especially on this subject, would have been much easier.

I knew very well that discussing the pregnant senior at Goshen High School with the Dassoris was a horrifying embarrassment for my mother. At the time, I didn't understand why. But the decision that came out of our parents' meeting that night was monumental. Loraine and I would be leaving parochial school. We would begin seventh grade at the local public school— Veraldi Junior High.

Of course, we were terrified about changing schools. We'd known after sixth grade something big was coming; but at least if we'd gone to Goshen Christian, we would have been moving up with the same twenty-one kids who'd been in our class since day one. There had been some comfort in the thought that we would all be making that transition together. Now, Loraine and I would be striking out on our own, into a totally unfamiliar environment, with kids neither of us knew. We were so nervous about the impending unknown that at first, one obvious advantage slipped by us.

We would get to wear real clothes.

Initiation

I'll never forget how excited I was the day we piled into Mrs. Dassori's car headed for the Paramus Park Mall, which was over an hour away in the neighboring state of New Jersey. Middletown, where we lived, was so rural back then we didn't even have a major department store. Oh, we had Lloyd's Shopping Center and Playtogs Discount Outlet, but neither Loraine nor I wanted to make our debut into public school wearing clothes from either of those places.

Middletown also had Tompkins, downtown on Main Street, but it was very expensive. We almost never went there, except when my mother was depressed. Even then, she never bought anything. Since both of us needed completely new wardrobes, our moms thought Tompkins would not be very practical. It was decided that we would have the most choices, and the most chances, at the big mall across the state line in New Jersey.

Paramus Park Mall was a huge, colorful, exciting place, and I'd only been there once before. But that other time, I was tagging along with Loraine and her family, a mere spectator. This time I was going to buy something. Lots of things, since my wardrobe up until that day had consisted of plaid wool uniforms and beat- up play clothes, and maybe one or two good dresses to wear to church on Sunday. I'd heard my mother and father discussing the trip over coffee that morning. I was in the next room, and they didn't know I could hear.

"She'll need at least five complete outfits, Hon. That's not going to be cheap."

I heard the loud clink of a spoon on a saucer. "How much room have we got left on the MasterCard?"

My mother's voice got quieter, and I couldn't hear her words.

After another mumbled exchange, I heard my father say, "Just make sure she gets nice clothes, not any of that trashy, hippie shit. I don't want my daughter looking like she's headed for a love fest."

Of course, I had no idea what kind of clothes I should be buying. Until I entered public junior high, it hadn't really seemed to matter what I wore, as long as the majority of me was covered and my clothes were clean. I entered the bright lights of Macy's department store that day with no expectations, only euphoric anticipation. The racks of colorful clothing seemed endless. I didn't even know where to start.

Loraine had a plan. She headed straight for the junior's section, marked by a sign hanging on chains from the ceiling. She started plucking outfits from one long rack, where plastic circles bearing numbers slid along between the hangers. We immediately began comparing the things we liked, chattering away like two little birds. I'd almost forgotten my mother was with me until I heard her voice, calling me from the other side of the rack.

"Fran! You'll have to look over here, Fran. I think your size might be over here."

I followed her to the other side. The little plastic circles on this side of the rack had more than one digit. Funny thing was, although the numbers were bigger, the number of choices between those little plastic circles seemed much, much smaller than on Loraine's side.

At first, I didn't understand how significant those numbers were. In my awe, gawking over all the bright colors and crisp fabrics, I wandered past the end of my section. Pulling out a particularly snazzy pair of denim bell bottoms with a multicolored flower embroidered on the back pocket, I held them up to show my mother.

"I like these, Mom. I can wear jeans to school now, right?"

My mom was shaking her head a little sadly as she replied, "Yes, you can wear denim, but I don't think those will fit you, honey."

I insisted on trying them on. Wiggle and strain as I might, there was just no way I was getting those size 14 jeans up over my pale, jiggly thighs. About the time I slunk out of my cubicle in the dressing room, Loraine was emerging from across the way, proudly sporting bellbottoms very similar to the ones I'd chosen, except in a lighter shade of blue. They hugged her hips and thighs all the way down to her knees before ballooning out wide over her shoes, the black shiny high-heeled ones she'd gotten on an earlier shopping trip with her mom. She stood in front of the three-way mirror near the entrance to the dressing room, admiring her image from every possible angle. She looked fabulous.

A sour feeling bubbled up into my chest. For the first time in my life, I felt like I could actually hate my best friend.

Loraine caught sight of the jeans my mother had carefully re-clipped onto the hanger in my hand as I tried to sneak by.

"Ooh, I like those! You gonna get 'em?"

"No," I said quietly, quickly adding, "I'm not really crazy about wearing embroidery on my butt. I'm gonna go look some more."

It was the longest day of my life. I finally agreed to try on things my mother had chosen for me, most of which came from the area across the aisle in the Women's section. Part of my dilemma was that the clothes in bigger sizes weren't as young-looking or fun. They seemed more like clothes my mother would wear: stretch polyester pants with elasticized waistlines and loose fitting, floral printed tunics. When I was twelve, Mom wasn't even as large as I was—yet. Out of modesty and deference for her age, she hid under the kind of clothing much, much older women usually wore.

The other issue that became apparent was that my height—or lack

31

thereof—didn't align with the size I needed to contain my bulbous form. By the time I found a blouse to span my ample bust and midsection, the shoulder seams hung halfway down to my elbows, and the cuffs covered my hands. The same went for the pants. Bellbottom denim was impossible to navigate in when a half-yard of the heavy cloth was dragging along the floor.

"I need some of those shoes like Loraine has, Mom," I whispered to my mother, not wanting Loraine to know just how jealous of her I had quickly become.

"You can't wear shoes like that, Fran. You know that. You've only been out of orthopedic shoes a couple of years."

Oh yes, the Buster Browns. Ever since I was old enough to walk, walking—and worse yet—buying shoes had been an issue. New shoes meant a trip to the tiny shoe store in the plaza on the edge of town. No one was ever in the store but us, a brightly lit, sterile space where an electronic ding-dong sounded when the door opened. The salesman's hair looked wet, and he smelled like he took a bath in Aqua Velva. With cold hands, he would press my white-socked foot down on an icy, flat metal tray with lines and numbers all over it. When I stood up, he would use both hands to bend my right foot, twisting my crooked ankle ever so gently to determine my size.

My shoes, up until just two years before that infamous shopping excursion, had been ugly, lace-up high tops that looked like granny shoes.

It was a sad fact: a kid who'd been born with a club foot wasn't strong or coordinated enough to walk in a high-heeled shoe. Although I walked almost normally by the age of twelve, I had still retained a slight slide to my right step, and both of my ankles were incredibly weak. I couldn't ice- or roller-skate. Sometimes my crooked ankle would fold out from under me when I stepped off a curb or down a stair. This hadn't been an issue too often, since both Loraine and I lived in one- story homes, and Mt. Carmel was all on one level. It was only when bounding down the bus steps too enthusiastically after school that I found myself grabbing frantically for the steel bar alongside.

I was a quick learner. I never once fell off the bus.

The tour we took of Veraldi Junior High a few days before had revealed the scary truth. It was a three-story building. My classes had always taken place in the same room. Not anymore. I would have to travel from one classroom to the next, multiple times daily, on different levels. An elevator, a stainless-steel freezer-looking door at the far end of the hallway from the office, was reserved for the handicapped kids. My mother informed me that I qualified. I silently vetoed the privilege.

No, I would be navigating the stairs, frantically in the seven minutes between the bells marking the end and beginning of classes. I would carry a heavy stack of books in my arms (backpacks hadn't quite become mainstream then), and there would be dozens of other kids jostling up and down the same flights.

My mother was right: I couldn't wear shoes like Loraine's.

The truth hit me that day, hanging in my chest like a hot anvil, under the glaring and unforgiving lights of Macy's. Bright lighting didn't disguise the truth, not one little bit, and had never really been my friend. I flashed back to the memory of that bare light bulb in Aunt Charlotte's upstairs hallway, and those nights when I struggled with truths too huge for a child to comprehend.

I was still struggling. I wouldn't be able to dress as fashionably as my slim and straight-legged friend. Loraine would get to wear cool shoes to make her look taller and leaner, even though she was already several inches taller than me. And unlike mine, her clothes came in single-digit sizes.

I was not only fat, but I was short; there didn't appear there was anything I could do to correct, or disguise, either mortifying condition.

As it turned out, we didn't get to buy anything that day. The fact hes were so much bigger than my best friend's became a very minor issue when we arrived at the checkout counter. We had spent hours picking out a cart full of clothes that my mother couldn't pay for. The stores didn't accept MasterCard, and that was the only money my mother had. Loraine and her mom had already paid and were waiting for us at the door. When they saw the commotion erupting at our cashier's stand, they had quietly slipped outside.

Aunt Charlotte stood with her hands on her hips, hooked nose in the air. Her eyes swept over me from head to toe as I stood there modeling the new outfit for my first day of public school.

"Isn't that velvet a little formal for a seventh grader? It looks like something she'd wear for Midnight mass, not the first day of school."

Mom knelt beside me, pinning the hem up so it hung straight all around and not too short--right below the middle of my kneecap. She had spent the better part of the last week at her sewing machine fashioning it.

"And what's she wearing with that?" Aunt Charlotte asked.

"We found her a satin blouse at Lloyd's. White satin. It looks beautiful against the red velvet," my mother answered.

My aunt's eyes finally found mine, staring up at her with wide, nervous eyes. I didn't understand why she seemed so disappointed in my mother's choice for an outfit for my first day of school—of *public* school. Charlotte's eyes took on a softer glow then, and she seemed a little sad.

Then she smiled and said, "You're gonna look gorgeous, Frannie. Don't you worry. You're gonna look simply beautiful."

My first day of public school was an early September day that broke all the temperature records in upstate New York. Although the maple trees lining the circular driveway in front of Veraldi Junior High glowed yellow and red, sunlight already boiled the fall air to steaming, as I climbed out of my parents' station wagon onto the sidewalk. I'd been granted pardon from riding the bus that first day of public school.

I started school in the skirt my mother made for me, even though Aunt Charlotte had tried to veto that decision. It was deep red velvet, one whose wide, flat waistband was already feeling damp as I climbed out of the back seat. I was wearing panty hose too, for the first time ever. The buzzy, tickly feeling when my knees brushed together made me feel very grown-up.

I arrived in homeroom, the launching and landing station where all students gathered to begin and end the school day. A tall, balding man with kind, green eyes stood between the chalkboard and his desk, smiling in a sympathetic way. MR. COX was scrawled on the board, in huge block letters scratched with white chalk.

Up until now, my only teachers had been nuns. The only man we ever interacted with at Mt. Carmel was Father Daly, and that was most often through a black screen in the confessional. Father Daly might have been a man, but you couldn't tell. He wore the same floor-length black robe the nuns did, just no veil over his short-cropped grey hair. This Mr. Cox was dressed like a man, wearing real clothes: dark green trousers, a shirt, and a tie.

On my first day at Veraldi Junior High, I experienced my first crush.

Mr. Cox had a soft, calming voice, and he laughed a lot, which made the skin around his eyes crinkle. He took attendance and then briefly went over a list of rules for behavior in the hallways. He asked if everyone had their class schedules. I glanced down nervously at the green and white striped paper on which mine had been printed.

"Does anyone have any questions?"

I had plenty, but I certainly wasn't about to raise my hand to ask. No one else did. So I waited until the bell rang and until everyone else had shuffled out the door into the hallway. Then I stopped in front of

Mr. Cox's desk.

"Mr. Cox, I'm sorry to bother you, but my first class is Music in room 218. Can you tell me where to find it?"

Mr. Cox looked up from the attendance book on his desk with a sympathetic smile.

"Of course. That's in the other side of the building, upstairs from the auditorium. It's kind of hard to find, though. I'll walk you there."

Those wrinkles and the shine of his bald scalp peeking through the strands of dark hair combed across made him seem much older than he might have been, but I didn't care. In the two minutes and thirty seconds that followed, with Mr. Cox escorting me to my first class, he transformed into my hero.

Loraine wasn't in my homeroom, and by the end of the first day, I realized that she and I only had two classes together: math and social studies. The new environment, all the strange kids, and being separated from me didn't seem to bother Loraine. The first I saw her all day she shuffled into math class chatting away with some girl I didn't know. She smiled in my direction but didn't come to sit by me. I figured it was because the desks around me were already occupied. Still, when Loraine took a seat in the far row right next to this new girl with the curly, red hair cascading down her back, I felt abandoned.

The air in the classrooms was very warm, especially near the window where the sun glared in, flashing off the long, satin sleeves of my blouse. The day had already seemed to last an eternity. I'd snagged a run in my pantyhose sliding into the desk in music class. The hole allowed my right knee to poke through when I sat down and got bigger every time I moved. When I stood up, a little bulbous patch of my thigh bulged in and out of the hole, especially when I climbed the stairs.

Even though it was hidden under my skirt, the sensation of that pulsating little blob punctuated every step. I was certain everyone I passed could see it. By lunchtime, the crotch of my hose had slipped down by several inches. That left puddles of flesh-colored folds around both of my ankles and allowed the tops of my sweaty thighs to rub and stick together with every move.

The air was even thicker in the stairwells where it seemed nine hundred kids were pushing past me all at the same time. I was too shy to talk to anyone. The only conversation directed toward me that first day was the comment from a girl buried under masses of curly, black hair who sat next to me in English class. She had exotic, slanted, dark eyes and was wearing bellbottom jeans with a sharp crease pressed all down the front of each leg. Her tight T-shirt had glitter glued over a bright geometric design. When she stared at me and smiled, I was instantly flattered. I thought maybe she wanted to be my friend.

"Nice outfit," she said.

I beamed with pride. "Thanks," I said, "My mom made my skirt."

"Oh really? I thought you found it in a dumpster," she laughed, loud and accusingly. "Is that why the button's in such a weird place?"

That's when I realized the pleats on the front of my skirt had shifted. The gold-toned button on the waistband, the one I'd watched my mother so painstakingly hand-stitch the night before, had crept around from the back and stuck out over my left hip.

By the end of that first day of public school, my new outfit had become a suit of armor. The velvet of my skirt was heavy and damp with sweat. The luxurious, napped fabric that had been smooth and elegant when I'd slipped it on that morning had deteriorated into a crinkled mass of flattened folds. My shiny blouse was crumpled and creased, and the top button continually and embarrassingly popped open. And Loraine seemed to have vanished into some imagined part of my parochial school past.

I took the bus home, fighting to contain my tears behind a trembling lip until I was safely down off that last step. My mother was there at the bus stop, waiting for me.

Her smile expressed pride and relief. "How was your first day, honey?"

I burst into tears and said nothing, sliding the monstrous stack of textbooks out of my weary arms into hers.

"Oh, you've snagged your hose. Don't worry about that. We'll get you some new ones. Was your skirt comfy? Did anybody notice how nice you looked?"

I couldn't bear to repeat the comment the girl in my English class had made, more out of embarrassment than to protect my mother's feelings.

"Loraine liked it," I croaked.

I felt her trembling hand on my shoulder then, and the lump in my throat grew even bigger.

"The first day is always the hardest, Fran," she said gently. "It'll get easier, I promise." She patted my shoulder as we walked together up the hill toward our house.

In the bathroom moments later, I peeled off my sweat-soaked clothes and caught sight of my reflection in the vanity mirror. The view was horrifying. The red dye from the velvet had bled onto my now-ruined blouse, soaking the stretched-out waistband of my pantyhose clear through to my skin. I appeared to be wearing a three-inch-wide crimson belt, even though I was completely nude.

Scrubbing with the soap and water in the shower didn't help one bit. The cherry color faded some, but still ringed my entire waistline, highlighting and drawing even more attention to my ample folds of flesh. The stain screamed a sad truth.

I was ugly, I was fat, and I'd been indelibly branded by a red, velvet skirt that looked like it came out of a dumpster.

Simply Beautiful

During those first few months of public school, a stark truth slammed my ignorantly innocent, twelve-year old mind: when everyone dresses the same, it levels the playing field. No matter how much I'd hated the pleats and plaid pinafore of Our Lady of Mt. Carmel, my identity there had been reasonably safe, sure, and predictable. I had known my place and how I was supposed to act. There was no need to worry about self- expression, at least in regard to wardrobe. In fact, individualism, as far as personal adornment, was not only discouraged, it was against the rules.

All that changed the day I started public school. I quickly discovered I didn't have a clue how to dress. Up until then, those decisions had been made for me. The playing field was no longer level. Once in the world of public school, I would be judged by the clothes I chose to wear, and my family's limited income would severely inhibit those choices.

I also had one more strike against me: I was overweight. In the highly competitive and brutal world of Twiggy-crazed, teenage girls, those pounds of fat became a most literal anchor.

We didn't own a scale. I knew there were an unspoken number of extra pounds that had doggedly followed my mother into her forties. Mom was just as happy no scale would remind her. When I'd gone shopping that day with Loraine and her family, I had no idea how much I weighed. I didn't really know what size I wore, or why it should matter. The very first time I ever remember stepping on a scale was at Loraine's house. By then, I was almost thirteen.

She was my best friend, and I was spending another Saturday night at her house. Her latest issue of Teen magazine had arrived, a subscription Loraine received every month and a privilege I envied. We perused the glossy magazine over our second bowl of strawberry ice cream, both sprawled belly-down across her bed with bare feet swaying over flannel-clad butts. The pale pink glow from her boudoir lamp matched the mounds in our bowls. I sucked thoughtfully on my inverted spoon.

"Whatcha gettin' for your birthday?" I asked.

We were both born in November, only two weeks apart, and those dates were coming up. This birthday would be a big one. We were getting ready to fall over the cliff into teen-land.

"Clothes. I always want clothes," was her reply.

Yeah, tell me about it was all that came to mind. I tempered my response—after all, Loraine was my only, best-forever-friend. Finally, I blurted out, "Well it's got to be a lot more fun to buy clothes when you wear a normal size."

Loraine's face popped up to meet mine, and I wasn't sure if it was indignation or pity in her eyes. "You could too, you know. You just have to go on a diet."

A diet. That was a four-letter word in my house. My mother struggled with weight on a daily basis ever since I could remember. She ate so little there were times I was afraid she'd starve to death. A diet seemed a horrible punishment. Mom was always swooning over some decadent pastry in the bakery, but seldom allowed herself more than one bite.

As luck had it, the feature in Loraine's issue of Teen was called "Healthy Eating." Inside an orange rectangle on the side of the page was a handy, little height and weight chart, especially designed for the growing teen.

"How tall are you?" Loraine asked. I shrugged.

The next half hour was a statistics course led by Loraine's mom, who stood us both up against the unfinished sheetrock lining their garage. She smudged small, pale pencil marks over the tops of our heads. Standing in bare feet on cold concrete, I suppressed a shiver as the rancid smell of motor oil made my nose wrinkle. It took a little calculation, since the cloth measuring tape from Mrs. Dassori's sewing kit was only five feet long. But in the end, I knew how tall I was, at least in that week before my thirteenth birthday: five foot, two and one-half inches.

We skipped back down the hallway, magazine and notebook in hand, eager to determine where we fell on the chart and find out how healthy we were. Loraine's weight fell comfortably within the parameters listed next to her height of five foot, six inches. She was apparently not only quite a bit taller than me, but quite a bit healthier.

The Dassori's bathroom always smelled like flowers, an aroma I thought emanated from the cabbage rose wallpaper. There were fancy, embroidered towels I'd learned quickly were not for drying my hands. Loraine sat cross-legged on the pink ceramic tile in her flannel pajamas, tapping her pencil on the notebook she had propped in her lap. My gut clenched the minute I stepped onto her pink scale, leaning forward to read the number over my ample bosom and belly.

"How much do you weigh?" she asked.

"Oh, this can't be right," I mumbled to myself.

I stepped on and off the scale three times secretly begging the number to change. I was shocked, mortified. I couldn't even read the dreaded number aloud.

"How much?" Loraine shrieked.

Frustrated, she jumped up to peer over my shoulder. The digits for me were illegible through my tear-filled eyes. I will never forget Loraine's wide-eyed gasp.

The next day, I went on a crash diet.

If *diet* was a four-letter word in my house, then *crash diet* was the equivalent of the F-word. Dieting was something old ladies did when their sugar or blood pressure was too high. That was my mother's excuse, on both counts, though dieting never seemed to help. Men didn't have to diet, and the only Italians whoever did were very sick, old ladies. Dieting was definitely not for a barely thirteen-year-old girl.

So mine was a secret. On schooldays, it was easy. I would push around the oatmeal or Honeycomb in my bowl, while Mom was busy at the counter making lunches. I dawdled patiently until Daddy went into the bathroom to shave. Hiding the contents of my untouched bowl wasn't difficult in a flip-top trash can that was perpetually full.

At school, I gave away the lunch my mom packed, since it was a sin to throw away good food. Most of the time, the taker was Donna Schwartz. She hovered at our table like a ravenous mongrel. It was hard to believe she was still hungry after watching her down the huge meal her mom had packed: an overstuffed sandwich dripping with mayonnaise, a Ring Ding, and not one, but two little bags of Ruffles potato chips. After a few weeks, I convinced my mother that I didn't want to brown bag anymore, much to Donna's dismay. I started bringing money to buy hot lunch. After that, my secret wardrobe savings account, the one I kept in an empty Chock Full O'Nuts can under my bed, began to grow.

Evenings were the hardest, since at our house, dinner was a family affair. By late afternoon, the house smelled heavenly. My mother was a great cook and prepared a fully balanced, steaming banquet every night. This was my father's rule: some main course of meat or fish, side of potato or pasta, always a green vegetable, and some kind of bread. Six o'clock, on the dot. At first, it was so hard to pretend I wasn't hungry. But I'd recall the image of those horrifying scale numbers, and my appetite disappeared.

"Mom, I've got a ton of homework tonight. And a math test tomorrow. Is it all right if I take my plate into my room?"

I directed the question to my mother, knowing full well it wasn't her call. She immediately glanced at Daddy, whose scowl alone could make my stomach sour. He frowned, his great heavy brows crawling toward his hairline. But we both knew I was armed with a powerful sword; good grades were almost more important to him than the family sitting down to dinner all together.

He brooded for just a minute, waiting as she ladled sauce over his rigatoni, before muttering, "It's all right, Hon. Let her go."

We didn't have a family pet then, a dog or a cat that might have benefited from my abstinence. I got very clever and discovered that the contents of a dinner plate flushed down the toilet just fine, whether it passed through the human digestive system or not. I'd make the sign of the cross and say a Hail Mary, as I washed the empty plate in the bathroom sink, since I knew I'd committed a sin. The truth was I had no willpower and couldn't limit myself to eating less. One bite of my mother's delicious cooking, and my resolve would dissolve. I found it was easier to just not eat at all.

Oh, I did eat some things. An apple on a Thursday at lunchtime, two bites of the fish Mom fried on Fridays. I'd allow myself a few spoonfuls of my mother's homemade chicken pastina soup on Monday, a dish I figured wasn't too fattening and probably had enough nutrients in it to keep me alive. Some nights, I'd eat all of my broccoli and maybe just a bite or two of the roast beef. No gravy, of course. But when my parents weren't around, I endeavored to eat nothing. Before long, the hunger pains disappeared, and the smell of food actually made me nauseous. I was well on my way to anorexia, my body adjusting to the twisted mindset alarmingly fast.

My father never paid much attention to me—at least physically—during those months. I was becoming a young woman. My body had begun to mature. His concern was my report cards, those documented evaluations of my intellect, which he scrutinized as though under a microscope.

But my body? I wonder if he figured ignoring that I was maturing into a young woman might stop it from happening. I dressed in such baggy clothes it would have been difficult to detect a difference unless you really looked. I guess he figured daddies weren't supposed to look at their daughters once their bodies began the transformation. Although I was surprised he didn't notice I was shrinking, I was also secretly relieved.

My father's younger sister suffered from—and eventually died of—anorexia nervosa. I remember Aunt Madeleine as bone-thin, pale, and jittery. I never saw her without her navy-blue stockings, ones she wore to cover ugly bruises from veins bursting under papery skin. By the time I was twelve, Aunt Madeleine had been trying to starve herself to death for almost twenty years. Unfortunately, she eventually succeeded.

My weight, or should I say, my fat folds, seemed to evaporate. Without a scale, it was impossible for me to track how much I was losing. But I knew my jeans didn't bind so much in the crotch when I sat down. The waistband eased looser every day. After a few weeks, the waistband started slipping down over my diminishing hips. I resorted to wearing my jeans unzipped, lapping one side over the other and fastening them with a huge safety pin I'd snatched from the basket on the edge of my mother's sewing table.

Every morning I got a thrill from feeling my clothes hang looser over a rapidly changing frame. I wore the same huge screen-printed T-shirts I'd been wearing all along. The same camouflage I'd used to disguise the generous folds around my middle now hid my lovely, shrinking secret.

Most perplexing was the reaction of the mirror in our bathroom: complete denial. I examined my body in detail every morning as I stepped out of the shower, but my reflection looked no different at all. I didn't look anything like Cheryl Tiegs on the cover of *Vogue* or Suzanne Somers on *Three's Company*. I wasn't strong, tall, and athletic like Loraine. To my eyes, the image in that mirror remained bulbous and unattractive, as ordinary but not quite as cute as the Pillsbury Dough Boy.

Six weeks after the first night I'd stepped on Loraine's scale, I stepped on it again. I'd dropped almost fifteen pounds. Loraine's mom heard the hoots and laughter coming from their only bathroom at the end of the hall. When we finally told her what all the celebration was about, Mrs. Dassori's face twisted into a disapproving scowl.

"Does your mother know you're on this diet?"

Did she? I know we never talked about it, but she must have noticed somewhere in time I'd stopped consuming entire bags of potato chips or gobbling down three of her homemade brownies when I came home from school. Sometimes, she'd even looked a little hurt when I refused to sample the cookies she'd just baked; but when I told her I was "trying to eat a little healthier," she just smiled and seemed proud of me.

My family lived very privately at home, even in a house far too small for four. I always undressed behind the locked door of our bathroom, since my younger brother and I shared a bedroom until I was sixteen. During those months, not even my mother saw me in my underwear.

I cowered in the doorway of Loraine's shiny, pink bathroom with her mother glowering at me.

"Well, does she?"

"Sort of," I answered quietly. It was hard for me to lie, since I was Catholic, and Hell loomed even larger than my father's certain rage.

"It's not healthy for you to lose weight this fast, Fran.

Especially at your age."

Unfortunately, I didn't take her advice, nor anyone else's, on the subject of dieting until a few months later. After four months of near starvation, spontaneous nosebleeds and fainting spells landed me in the emergency room of Horton Memorial Hospital. In my own misguided teenage mind, it was all worthwhile. Three months and twenty-two days after my crash diet began, I finally fell within the "normal" weight range for my age and height, at least according to Teen magazine. I'd lost a total of forty pounds.

My mother's reaction to my brush with anorexia was a paradox. At first, of course, she was horrified, feeling guilty, I'm sure, that she hadn't realized what I'd been doing to myself for the past few months. Slowly though, I sensed her mixture of pride and trepidation at my dubious accomplishment. Her daughter wasn't a pudgy kid anymore, and from under the baby fat had emerged a curvaceous, attractive young woman. I know she was proud of me, but somehow the "new me," and how the world would surely notice, made her worry.

Once the drama of the E.R. visit was behind me, and a doctor was monitoring my "new healthy regime," a new wardrobe was in order. My jeans were, by then, so big I couldn't even keep them up with pins anymore. It was time I stopped hiding under those baggy screen-printed tees.

"We'll go to that new store, Fran. I heard they have very reasonable prices. And a nice selection, too."

White's Department Store hadn't been open more than a few months. The store was huge, an obvious play on the Macy's theme, and one our little town desperately needed. That Saturday, the skies of upstate New York were March grey. Mountains of dirty snow still blanketed the base of each light pole in the parking lot. But inside, spring was in the air. The windowless space washed blindingly bright, and fake cherry blossom-covered twigs decorated every display. Pale mannequins wore bathing suits, scraps of bright fabric that covered little more of their bodies than did the broad band of black eyeliner around their sightless, almond-shaped eyes.

"You'll need a nice dress for Easter this year. We're going to Grandma's. Everyone will be there."

"I'll need a new bathing suit soon, too. I want a bikini."

My mother frowned. "Your father won't allow a bikini, and you know that."

"But Mom, I've worked so hard to wear one!"

Mom shook her head, tsk-ing. "We still have to live with your father."

We hadn't even made our way into the junior's department when we both saw it. *The dress.* It was hanging on a rack all by itself, emanating a heavenly glow. A form-fitting style, my mother called it "princess- seamed." The velvety fabric was white. Otherwise unadorned, the dress had pearl buttons tracing the center seam all down the front. It was simply beautiful. My mother and I both stopped in our tracks before the display.

"But it's white. White will make me look fat, won't it, Mom?"

My mother's grin screamed pride. "You're not fat anymore. Come on. Try it on."

The first trip I took two sizes into the changing room, since I had no idea where to start. The last time I'd bought clothes, I had barely squeezed into a size 16. As I slipped the 14 over my head, my heart was racing. My mother pulled the zipper up the back.

"Oh, this is way too big," she said, her voice an octave higher with excitement. "Try on the 12."

That one was too big as well, hanging over my newly shrunken form as though the zipper was still undone. My mother was getting giddier every minute.

"You wait here. I'll go see if they have a smaller size," she called over her shoulder as she whisked away.

I waited alone in the cubicle under the bright, unforgiving lights of White's-wannabe-Macy's in my white bra and pink panties and nothing else. I timidly examined my reflection in the mirror. This one was no better than the one at home, reflecting a body no different to my eyes. My brain knew I was smaller, but my eyes weren't registering the change. My mother returned with another white dress hanging over her arm.

"Here, try this one on."

When she slid the zipper up along my spine a chill scurried down in the opposite direction, tingling all the way to my toes. The dress fit and like a glove. It wasn't tight but didn't bag or hang loose anywhere. When I turned to face the mirror, I didn't recognize the young woman who gawked back at me. She was really me.

"It's an 8. You're a size 8 now, Fran." Mom's eyes filled. Her fears had somehow been overcome. My curves were evident, even plainly on display. But since they were swathed in puritanical white, it was okay. I looked simply—innocently—beautiful.

My mother was in the midst of her daily telephone conversation with her sister Charlotte. "You should see the dress we got for Fran for Easter, Sis." I could hear my aunt's voice as it sprayed through the earpiece, but I couldn't quite make out the words. "It's white," my mother replied. "She looks so beautiful in it."

Again, my mother was silent as Aunt Charlotte chattered on. I so now wish I could have heard exactly what she said.

"No, Sis. No hat. She won't need one." After another lull, my mother replied adamantly. "She doesn't need a hat for Easter Mass. I have a white lace hankie to pin on her head. Just like I do."

A pang of disappointment zinged through me. For the first time in my life, I thought perhaps I was skinny enough, pretty enough, confident enough to wear something a little daring. I would have loved to add a hat to the ensemble for our Easter outing. One with a wide brim, white to match my dress, but maybe with some brilliant fuchsia roses, perhaps a bit of organza or lace.

In the end, it really didn't matter. I was thirteen, with a brand-new body, and more pride than sense with which to flaunt it. My wings were still wet.

I didn't realize it then, but in the self-image department, I still had a long way to go.

Hugs

My transition from chubby, Catholic schoolgirl to curvaceous, public school teenager spurred my father into a decision I'd been prodding him for since I was old enough to talk. I was horse crazy, though where the obsession came from, nobody knows. The two or three summer riding lessons when I was eight years old were as close as I'd ever gotten to the dream of owning my own horse.

That first tumultuous year in public junior high was finally over. One glorious June morning, I stumbled sleepily out into the kitchen where my mother stood at the stove, stirring oatmeal. My father sat in his usual spot at the head of the table, a newspaper fanned open before him and a cigarette burning in the amber ashtray to his right. I assumed my assigned seat, a screech from the chair's leg on the linoleum earning me a dour glance from Daddy.

Everything seemed perfectly normal.

"Sit down, Hon," my father glanced up at Mom. "We can eat later." His tone was ominously serious. I mentally thumbed through the events of the week – had I earned a bad grade? No, my final report card had been stellar. I was pretty sure I'd done all the chores my mother had assigned. I hadn't smacked my little brother lately, though I'd wanted to. What on earth was up?

Mom lifted the battered aluminum coffee pot off the gas stove burner, refilling my dad's cup, then her own. She looked so fresh and pretty, even at this early hour, in her pale pink housecoat, her hair neatly pinned into a bun at the nape of her neck. Her suppressed smirk wasn't nearly as scary as my father's expression.

The moment stretched out as my gaze darted from Mom to Dad and back again. She replaced the coffee pot and sat, stirring cream into her cup. The clinking of metal on ceramic rang unusually loud. She clicked the spoon down on the saucer, then perched both elbows on the table, resting her chin on clasped hands. She was struggling to suppress a smile. How odd.

My father took a deep draw on his freshly lit cigarette. "Your mother and I have decided to buy you a horse." His words came out in a billow of smoke that drifted around his head, as diaphanous and ethereal as what he'd just said.

I choked, sputtering on a mouthful of juice.

"What? How? We don't have a barn. Where would we keep a horse?"

"We'll keep him in the garage."

The absurdity of the idea didn't cause me a second's hesitation. I was being offered my dream. You don't question a dream.

My father, with his deadpan serious face, in his droning monotone, continued, as though his words weren't about to change my entire life.

"There are a couple of ads here in the paper. Under Livestock for Sale." He sipped his coffee, took another draw on his cigarette. "Eat your breakfast. We'll go take a look at a few this morning."

And so, yes, my first horse really did live in our garage. A golden palomino, I named him Brandy. My older brothers constructed a pine-planked stall in the one-car garage attached to our house. The garage had been an add-on, thereby encasing two of the home's windows. The one in our single bathroom had been boarded over. The other, a double-width storm window, opened into my bedroom.

Funny, but it never seemed strange back then. If I pushed aside

52

the drape and looked out my bedroom window, my horse looked back. Every morning, from that summer on, I awoke to a sweet, strange music: rustling of wood shavings, stomping of hooves, snorting and blowing. Many times during those first few weeks, floating in the hazy place between awake and asleep, I thought I must be dreaming. What a wondrous revelation when I realized my dream had come true.

Brandy could hear me, too. If I coughed or sneezed, he replied with a soft nicker or impatient whinny. Once my mattress springs creaked, bedtime was officially over. Brandy knew I was up, and it was time to eat.

His feeding ritual became my daily mantra. Most mornings I greeted him still clad in my pajamas. The heavy, old, wooden garage door, definitely past its prime, squealed horrifically as it was raised or lowered. Brandy grew accustomed to the din, like Pavlov's dog. He knew the ear-splitting sound meant impending food.

That euphoric summer, I began each day with my nose buried in a swatch of fragrant timothy hay as I carried it to Brandy's stall. I swooned to the sound of him crunching his first mouthful of oats. Even though I'd only had three riding lessons in my life, the activity seemed to come naturally. Every sunny day, I outfitted Brandy with the western saddle and bridle we'd bought along with the horse and took off down our country road, beyond the paved edge where the yellow and black sign warned *Dead End.*

There was no dead end for Brandy and me. We spent hours exploring the miles of unpaved roads winding through the hilly woods.

On rainy days, I wielded currycomb and dandy brush, polishing his coat until it shone like burnished gold. I braided ribbons in his long, white mane. I taught him how to give me a hug, wrapping me into his neck with his giant, soft-eyed head. Some days we just hung out together. I'd take my current book—*National Velvet* or *Black Beauty* or the like—and climb up onto the top bale of hay in the corner.

Or I'd talk to him. Brandy was a very good listener. I was as happy as I'd ever remember being in my short life.

But summer ended, and school recommenced, somewhat complicating the job of taking care of my horse. Even though I had three brothers, they never expressed any interest in their sister's giant pet. Seldom, if ever, did they volunteer to assist in his care. Which was okay—at least they'd built the stall where he lived.

That winter, I learned my first physics lesson. Or was that chemistry? No matter. We lived in upstate New York, where winters can be tough. Where a five-gallon bucket of water freezes through solid when left overnight in an unheated garage. Even one where a 900-pound animal resides.

I set my alarm clock early, dreading the formidable task before me. It took fifteen minutes to suit up: boots and coat, hat and mittens. Then I trudged through sometimes knee-deep snow down the length of our house to the garage. Just raising the door was a daunting task, since the ancient rollers ran on rusted, dented channels. The din, some mornings, could have wakened the dead.

Brandy waited patiently as I heaved and tugged with both hands, finally convincing the heavy old door to inch up just far enough so I could duck underneath. When it was windy, I crawled in on my hands and knees. I worried the chill whipping in would reach my precious horse, even wrapped as he was in the heaviest, quilted blanket I could talk my dad into buying.

Dawn was still midnight-black during Northeast winter mornings when I snapped on the lights. Brandy's warm breath sent little cloudbursts into the frigid air as he blinked at the sudden brightness. To the rumbling of his soft nickers, I scooped grain into a bucket and tossed him some hay. That was the easy part. The real challenge, I knew, still lay before me.

I was a bit anal about the cleanliness of my horse's drinking water. I couldn't imagine drinking dirty water, so how could I rest easy if Brandy's wasn't sparkling clean as well? His five-gallon bucket got emptied, scrubbed, and refilled twice a day, regardless of weather.

With numb fingers hindered by hay-flecked mittens, I fumbled with the metal snap holding the bucket fast to the side of Brandy's stall. It was white, recycled plastic with a scratched and peeling Dunkin Donuts label declaring "Raspberry Filling" on the side. Since Brandy never drank more than half of what I'd left the night before, by morning I knew the plastic mold would be clogged with a solid, twenty-pound chunk of ice.

I rolled the bucket outside, kicking it along with the toe of my boot. Like a giant ice cube tray, sometimes the kinetic energy was enough: as the sides flexed, the block would slide out. Other times were more difficult. I resorted to standing on the bucket's curved exterior, balancing with both feet in the pre-dawn chill, in the dark, in the snow, bouncing my entire body weight up and down to convince the plastic to let loose of its winter sculpture.

From November to April, our front yard transformed into an Antarctic Stonehenge. Cylindrical blocks of varying heights, depending on how thirsty Brandy had been the night before, formed the display. Sometimes the blocks imprisoned strands of golden-green hay or nuggets of bronze oats. As I trudged up the driveway from the bus stop on cold, clear afternoons, the flashes of pale, winter sunlight shooting through the ice were blinding.

Distance: exactly twenty-three steps divided our front door and the entrance to the garage. The trip back was never shorter, always exactly twenty-three steps. But carrying a two-thirds-full bucket of water, in deep snow or high winds, proved challenging. Water sloshed over the edge, soaking my jeans and filling my boot. Some mornings I thought surely I would die before I got a full bucket of clean water back into Brandy's stall. The only way I made it was by counting the steps.

Brandy was always so grateful. As soon as I slid the bucket under his door, he turned to face me, wearing a mouthful of hay like a beard, waiting patiently as I fastened the snap to the bucket's bale. Then he'd dunk his big, soft muzzle into the steaming water, slurping loudly. It was always just a sip or two. When he raised his head, water dripped from his whiskered chin. His dark eyes said the words clearly: thank you.

So, what inspired my father to finally give in and buy me a horse? Was he tired of hearing me beg? Feeling overly generous? Maybe, but I don't think so. I believe his decision was strongly influenced by the events of the previous year: my transition into public school with all its potential "bad influences"; my loss of forty pounds and the emergence of a shapely young woman's body; the commencement of my menses, which no doubt my mother had shared with him; and my mention of the cute boy who sat next to me in math class.

Today, parents speak openly with their teenagers, giving advice on safe sex and how to avoid pregnancy. Some even start their daughters on birth control pills when their cycles begin. My father took a subtler, oblique route.

If I buy her a horse, she won't think about boys . . . yet.

Was Brandy a symbolic chastity belt? Maybe. If so, my father's plan worked. At least for the next several years.

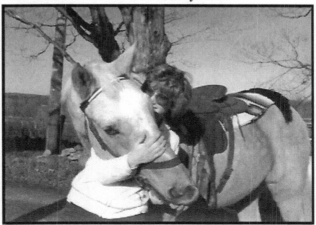

The Trouble with Hats

With the help of a continued healthy diet, along with the physical exercise my horse provided, I managed to stay relatively slim and fit throughout my high school years. My problem, by the time I entered my senior year, was not wardrobe choices.

Or maybe, in a way, it was. I fought a constant battle between dressing appropriately, in the eyes of my parents, and fashionably in the eyes of my then very counter-establishment peers. It was 1974. Hot pants and bellbottoms, sequined bandeaus and Spandex—"bubble" tops—defined the fashion world. Every few weeks over the summer, Mom tried to squeak enough out of the budget to buy me a new outfit for school.

I loved when Aunt Charlotte came along. I came home one day from a shopping expedition, anxious to model my newest outfit—a clingy bubble top tucked into hip-hugger bellbottoms with a wide, patent leather belt riding low on my shapely hips. I thought my father was going to have a heart attack.

"She will not—*will not*—leave the house dressed like that. She looks like a floozy," he declared, glaring at my mother.

Mom hadn't been too thrilled with my choices either; but whenever Aunt Charlotte was along, I had an ally.

My mother took my aunt shopping every Tuesday. First groceries. Then, as my Charlotte called it, *discretionary shopping* commenced. I loved summers because I got to tag along every week.

But school was about ready to begin, and I still needed a new winter coat. I was heading into my senior year of high school.

"You know, you really need a hat to finish off that ensemble." Aunt Charlotte was studying me with narrow-eyed scrutiny.

I was modeling my choice for a new winter coat. It was navy blue wool.

"It's like your old pea-coat, Sis," Mom said. She was fondling the coat's lapel between two fingers.

Her sister snorted and threw Mom a disgusted look. "Those things had no shape. This one has style—just look at how it fits her." She stepped back and tossed her hands in the air. "That cinched waistline and wide collar—they really show off her figure."

Lloyd's Department Store was the original Super Wal-Mart, years before Sam Walton came up with idea. Lloyd's was a sprawling, single floor complex on the rapidly expanding edge of downtown Middletown, just a block or so from the new Orange Plaza Mall. Lloyd's started out as a simple grocery store but, little by little, Ed Lloyd expanded, adding everything from Housewares to Gardening to Toys. A boost for the local economy, the Shoe Department was the first place my older brother ever worked, and my first job at sixteen was in Music. Lloyd's brought in an expansive soft- goods line as well and could outfit a person from Millinery to Shoes—all at heavily advertised discount prices.

My coat came from their Ladies' Wear department: a sturdy, navy blue woolen in the new "midi-length" that just brushed the top of my ankle.

"But you'll need a scarf to cover your neck—that V is pretty deep." Mom was always more concerned about my catching cold than any attention.

Lloyd's Millinery department offered a wide variety of accessory items. It didn't take long for me to spy bright stripes from the bottom of a stack of colorful knitted scarves. The blue was just the right shade.

The acrylic yarn was soft, and the scarf wasn't very wide; but it was long, plenty long enough to wrap once around my neck, with enough extra to fling over one shoulder.

"That's a sassy look," Aunt Charlotte said. "Ooh, I love that. But you still need a hat."

"Sis," my mother was shaking her head, "you and your hats." Mom was staring at her hands, as she picked at a hangnail. She never wore a hat, not even in church. My mother was more comfortable bobby-pinning an embroidered hankie to her head than perching anything on top of her carefully confined bun or braids that might attract attention. But when Aunt Charlotte was along, Mom seldom argued.

Aunt Charlotte helped me choose a classy, wide- brimmed fedora very much in vogue. Until the holidays drew near that year, I wore it just the way it was, with a dyed-to-match feather sticking up out of the grosgrain ribbon band. After Thanksgiving, I decided to make the style my own.

I fastened one side of the brim up with a sparkly snowman pin fashioned out of cheap rhinestones. A three-dollar find at *Keepsakes*, the costume jewelry kiosk in the center of the mall, I bought it with my first paycheck. I'd landed a part-time job at Sullivan's, the fancy department store that anchored the new Orange Plaza.

The outfit was young and cocky and carefree, and it made me feel just that way. Whenever I wore it, I felt strikingly pretty. I'll never forget the gleam in Charlotte's eyes when she saw me all dressed up in my new ensemble for the first time.

"Now you're dressed—there's nothing like a hat to polish off an outfit. And to turn heads," she said with a grin and a wink.

***

I met Harry right after Halloween. He manned that jewelry kiosk outside of Sullivan's. In the toy department, I spent the pre-holiday season fighting off throngs of frantic parents in search of toys for their precious little ones, toys whose names I couldn't even pronounce, let alone locate in the colorfully jumbled aisles. After enduring four of my eight hours of the Saturday shift, I was definitely ready for some lighthearted conversation.

Keepsakes was one of the seasonal island businesses that dotted the center aisle of the mall for a transient few months before Christmas. I'd first met Harry during one of the mid-afternoon breaks that old Sydney Sullivan graciously allowed his holiday help. A few weeks before our first date, I'd worn my new, navy wool coat and matching fedora for the first time and had set out into the mall to enjoy my respite. I heard an odd voice toss a comment over the glass partition, as I whisked past on my way to Orange Julius to grab a hot dog.

"Hey there, pretty lady. Charming chapeau," an odd voice called after me.

That was the first time I ever spoke to Harry, over the top of the display case that contained him. That was our only meeting place until the night he showed up for our date at my house, just two weeks later. I never realized just how short he was. He couldn't have been more than five-foot-three, including the height of his clunky, thick-bottomed shoes. I hadn't noticed the Frankenstein shoes until he stepped into the light of our kitchen to introduce himself to my parents.

In my family, the "meeting" was a necessary ritual. I was not allowed a date with anyone who wouldn't walk in our front door and shake hands with my father—at least, that's what I'd been told. In truth, I'd only ever had one date before Harry. That young man, John, knew my parents before he even met me. He'd sold them a new refrigerator from the appliance store where he worked. The only reason I'd been allowed to date John—he was five years older than me—was because my father knew him and liked him. And John probably gave him one hell of a deal on that Frigidaire.

Harry was the first "stranger" I'd ever dated.

If I'd only known how applicable that adjective would turn out to be.

"So, where are you taking my daughter tonight, Harry?" My father was folding his lower lip between his thumb and index finger, one furry eyebrow lifted.

"It's called the Hilltop. My best friend is the head chef there. The food is quite good."

Harry's voice squeaked as though he'd been sucking on a helium balloon. My father's silence preceded the amused expression flashing across his face. Then his bushy eyebrows both came to life, crawling up toward his thinning hairline.

"The Hilltop. Hmm. I've lived here pretty much all my life, Harry, and I've never heard of that restaurant. Where is it?"

"It's on Rt. 211. Not far. I'll have your daughter home right on time, Mr. Del Negro. Don't worry."

Harry's voice didn't strike me as unusual, since every time I'd stopped to chat with him in the mall, he'd sounded exactly the same. At first, I thought maybe he had a cold or a sinus condition; but after the second week of our daily conversations, I'd come to accept that his voice pretty much matched the rest of him—small, squeaky, and strange. In some weird way, he was almost cute, in an innocent, little boy way. One thing was certain: he knew all the right things to say to a girl to make her feel all grown up and special. Most importantly, he seemed harmless. At least to me. I was only seventeen.

Standing in our kitchen, waiting for my father's nod of approval, the sweat on my palms started to make them itch. I busied myself with my coat, sliding the sturdy wool over my shoulders and snugging the sash tight around my waist. I tossed my striped scarf boldly over one shoulder and finished the ensemble by donning my hat. Then, clutching the confidence my outfit gave me, I sashayed out the door on the arm of a weird, little man I hardly knew.

By the time I'd ducked into Harry's Dodge Omni, I wondered how I'd ever gotten myself into this. I really didn't know this guy. And once I was alone with him in his toy-like car, conversation with Harry seemed much more difficult than when we were standing in the center of the mall with a junk jewelry counter protecting me from him.

"Are you hungry, Fran? You're in for a treat tonight. Hans is an excellent chef."

"Yes, I am. I didn't have time for lunch today. Is this restaurant new, Harry?"

"Oh no. It's been there for years. It's right across the highway from the mall."

I searched my memory of that stretch of road. I'd grown up in Middletown, but I didn't recall any restaurant there.

"Where exactly?"

"It's up on the hill, right next to the Middletown Motel."

It was my eyebrows' turn to come to life. "Oh?" "Yes, my friend Hans, he's a graduate of the New York Culinary Institute. He runs The Hilltop. Hans and I have been friends for a very long time."

Maybe it was just a coincidence that the restaurant was attached to a motel. After all, many fancy hotels have five-star restaurants. One doesn't necessarily have to be renting a room there to have a nice dinner. It was just that I never considered the Middletown Motel of the same caliber as a Hilton or Marriott.

I was thoroughly familiar with this establishment. When I was a little kid, my dad's sister stayed there every summer with my cousin. For a week every August, they came up from Brooklyn for a "vacation in the country." I'd spent many an afternoon wrestling in the blue water of their pool with my little brother and my cousin Chris.

Our favorite game was diving for pennies, which we did for hours on sunny, hot afternoons. My dad would toss the coins into the eight-foot deep end, and we spent more time under the water than swimming on top, until our skin was scarlet and sore, and my hair was bleached from mouse-brown to *Sun-In* blonde. The Middletown Motel, at least when I was a kid, was a very respectable, middle income motel.

But as Harry turned his car onto that familiar steep, winding drive, the place didn't seem nearly as friendly or fun as I'd recalled. It was dark, and it was winter, so the parking lot was nearly empty. I never remembered eating at what Harry now referred to as their gourmet restaurant. Adding to my anxiety was that I noticed The Hilltop, as we drove by on the way to a parking space, appeared to be closed.

"Uh, Harry, I don't think the place is open. Today is Monday. It's says on their sign there that they're closed on Mondays."

"Don't worry yourself about that, my dear. Hans is cooking especially for us tonight. We'll have the place all to ourselves."

A chill crawled up my spine as Harry's sudden condescending use of "my dear" struck a note of dissonance. When Harry pounded on the locked glass door, it didn't take more than a minute for Hans to appear, thumping across the carpeted floor with a massive ring of keys in one hand. He was a huge man, Lurch-like, and sported a blond buzz cut to go with his white chef's button-up. The lights in the burgundy-carpeted dining room were dimmed but failed to disguise the fact that every table in the place was empty. Most of the chairs were propped upside-down on bare tabletops.

There was only one table set, tucked into the corner underneath a latticework display of wine bottles covered with artificial vines. As Hans pulled out a chair for me, I noticed purple and green plastic grapes nestled among the faded silk leaves, and they were covered in a fuzz of gray dust. But the table was freshly swathed in pristine white linen, several cut-glass votive holders lighting its circular surface.

"Now you can order anything on the menu, my dear, but Hans is really best with cuts of meat. His steak au poivre is amazing."

Harry ordered a Jack and Coke, and plain Coke for me—without asking. I would have preferred a diet version, but I was so disoriented by the peculiarity of my situation that I was afraid to protest. Hans brought the drinks and filled our cut-crystal water glasses from a frosted stainless pitcher that he cradled between two white napkins as we waited for the appetizers to arrive. My appetite by then had disappeared.

Harry kept reaching across the starched surface toward me with his tiny, pale hand. His fingers reminded me of those on unborn fetuses I'd seen in the pictures of a recent Time magazine article called "The Miracle of Life." The shrimps of his appetizer course looked gargantuan between digits that matched them— smooth, pink, and waxy. Everything about Harry was small and slight, and I drew some comfort in the thought that I probably outweighed him. Even his short, black curls were boyish, accented by an apparently not- yet-deepened-by-hormones voice. His black rimmed glasses were too big on his face. But as the conversation progressed, I slowly realized that Harry was not as young as he appeared.

"How long have you worked for the jewelry company, Harry?"

"Oh, since 1964. I started with them right after high school."

The current year was 1974. The math was easy: the shock of realization a bit more difficult.

"So, you're, uh, how old?"

"I'll be twenty-eight next month."

I choked on my water. As I dabbed the cloth napkin to my chin, I could feel a lozenge-sized piece of ice slide down my throat, all the way down to my stomach.

"You certainly don't look that old," I sputtered. "Why, thank you, my dear." When Harry smiled, his cheeks bumped the oversized frame of his glasses, making them wiggle. He reached across the table again, sending my own hands to hide in my lap.

It didn't seem possible that I'd once had so much to talk about with this strange, little man standing in the center aisle of the mall; now alone with him, I couldn't start a conversation no matter how I tried. He seemed to dodge every question I asked about his family or background with some vague dismissal.

Harry had no interest in talking about my dog, my cat, or my horse, even though he'd seemed fascinated by those stories when we chatted in the mall. When I started telling him about my plans for college, he yawned. He wasn't nearly as charming as he had seemed when standing in his kiosk either, showing off all the glittery baubles he had displayed on black velvet under the glass. This night he just continued to stare at me with an ominously gleeful expression, one that was now giving me the creeps. I grew even more uncomfortable when Hans came out carrying a silver coffee urn, hovering over me and glaring down as he poured with strange, glowing eyes.

I don't even remember what I ordered for dinner. My appetite had vanished the minute Hans locked the door behind us. I tried to avoid eye contact with Harry, so he wouldn't realize just how frightened I had become. When Hans asked if we wanted dessert, my head was shaking no, but Harry insisted I try their "fabulous" New York cheesecake.

In my navy-blue, leather handbag, there was plenty of change to make a phone call, along with seven rolls of pennies in the bottom that made it weigh three times what it appeared to. They were strategically placed there, able to become a weapon if need be. Although I felt quite sure the penny-flail could take Harry down, there would still be Hans to contend with. I excused myself to the ladies' room, hoping to find a pay phone in the vestibule. No phone was within view. I returned to the table; as Hans poured my third cup of coffee, I toyed with the untouched strawberry cheesecake, my mind racing as fast as my heart. Remembering again the locked glass doors, I realized the severity of my predicament.

I tried very hard to steady the tremor I knew was quivering my voice. "So, Harry, where exactly do you live?"

He was busy mashing the last bits of his own cheesecake into the raspberry syrup that laced the bottom of the plate. His fork looked like a tiny pitchfork in his hand.

"I have an apartment in Virginia, but I'm not usually there much. Keepsakes keeps me on the road a lot."

He paused, gently laid his fork down on the edge of his plate and leaned toward me. His eyes had taken on a suspiciously evil gleam.

"I'm up this way quite a bit. Every major holiday, in fact. I always stay here at the hotel." A grin transformed his face into a crazed, villainous caricature.

That's when it hit me: Harry had a room. No doubt it was right down the hall from where we sat. The key he retrieved from his pocket, after leaving a wad of folded bills on the table for Hans, wasn't his car key.

"Uh, Harry, I really need to be getting home."

"Oh, certainly you have time for a glass of wine. Hans has packed us a chilled bottle and a couple of glasses to take back to my room. He couldn't serve you here in the restaurant, of course, you being underage and all."

"So, you do realize that I'm only seventeen?" I tried hard to sound confident, even adamant. "I *just turned* seventeen, you know."

"Yes, I'm well aware of that. But don't worry yourself, my dear. If you were under sixteen, then we might have a problem." He stifled a chuckle. "But we're fine. Just fine."

I cleared my throat and shifted in my seat, fixing my stare rigidly on the dusty grapes behind Harry's head. There were purple grapes, and there were green ones. I took a slow breath and spoke directly to the grapes.

"I'm only seventeen, and I know I've told you my last name. You must realize that my family is Italian. My father is from New York City, old school Italian. Very old school."

A little span of silence followed as Harry began rubbing his hands together, one over the other, as if they were cold.

"No, I didn't realize that."

"He still has a lot of friends in the city, Harry. As a matter of fact, my uncle and my cousin still live there. Did I tell you about my cousin Chris? He's a bouncer for a bar down in Bay Ridge." I paused, grasping desperately for details. "Chris is a body builder. He works out in the same gym as Lou Ferrigno. You know, the Incredible Hulk? He's actually one of his bodyguards." Although this interesting bit of trivia was true, I'd never mentioned it to anyone before. It had never seemed important.

"Is that a fact?"

Harry's voice was quiet, followed by another period of silence during which he kept switching his gaze from his wormy hands—he rubbed one over the other faster and faster—to the lighted porthole window in the swinging door to the kitchen.

"I think you better take me home, Harry. My father will be very unhappy if I am late. Very unhappy."

"It's early. I told him I've have you home by ten. It's barely eight o'clock."

"I'd like to go home now. Dinner was very nice, but now I'd like you to take me home."

I stood up from the table and grabbed my coat off the back of my chair, swaying only slightly, although my legs felt like rubber. Although Harry made no move to get up, I methodically began to dress for the cold ride home.

It felt good to cover up, layering my scarf across my chest, cinching the belt of my coat securely around me. Harry remained seated for another minute, then huffed quietly as he slid the key with the plastic tag imprinted with the number "42" back into his breast pocket. As I started to arrange my hat on my head, I stopped. I clutched it instead to my chest.

"You're sure you won't stop in for just one glass of wine? I have a very nice suite, you know."

"No. I want to go home. Now."

The kitchen door flung open, and Hans appeared, flashing Harry a bewildered glance as he fumbled with the keys to unlock the door. Once we were outside, the sharpness of the icy air felt wonderful in my lungs. I remember thinking, I'm out, I'm safe. But the fact was I still had to depend on Harry to get home. The Middletown Motel sat atop a lonely hill, at least a mile away from any activity I might have run to. I could see the lights of Orange Plaza down across the four-lane highway, but they seemed small and far away. I glanced around the entrance to the building, but there was no pay phone in sight.

Harry didn't say a word as he unlocked the passenger door and opened it for me. He walked around, got in and started the engine, and it was then I noticed that he had donned a pair of black, leather gloves. They made his hands seem huge. He perched both black mitts on the steering wheel and sat there, staring ahead, but not saying a word. I assumed he was waiting for the engine to warm up.

The temperature had dropped well below freezing, and frost had formed along the bottom of the windshield. An icy coating had grown several inches above where the motionless wiper blades sat, and Harry wasn't tall enough to see over the frosted edge. The light from the sconces along the side of the building sparkled in a golden snowflake pattern through the frost.

Finally, Harry turned to stare at me again, his eyes suddenly appearing huge behind his glasses.

"Are you sure you won't change your mind, Fran? I have a really nice room. I even rented us a couple of movies."

"Just take me home, Harry."

"I know you wouldn't regret it. I may be a little guy, but I really do have a lot to offer."

At that moment, I felt his icy glove close around my wrist. Before I realized what was happening, he had grabbed my hand and was pulling it toward him. Then he pressed it down onto his crotch. Thin fabric was warm over a hard bulge underneath.

The wave of nausea almost overtook me, and I swallowed hard as I snatched my hand away.

"Take me home, Harry. If you don't take me home right now, my father will make very sure that you regret it."

During the five-mile drive back to my house, neither one of us spoke. I sat hunched in my seat as far toward the door as I could get, both hands stuffed in the pockets of my coat. That hand was balled up and stiff, and I held it as far away from my body as the lining of my pocket would allow. It felt alien, contaminated, and I couldn't wait until I could scald it with hot water and scrub it with disinfectant. When Harry's car crunched onto our driveway, I threw open the door before we'd even come to a full stop.

I leapt out; but just before the door slammed shut, I heard Harry call, "I'll be in town again next month, just before Valentine's Day. I'll give you a call."

***

I never got the chance to tell Aunt Charlotte about my perilous night with Harry, the date that might never have occurred had Harry not noticed my hat. By the time I was in my late teens, Charlotte's heart began its rapid decline. It seemed she got sick and deteriorated quickly. Maybe I was just too seventeen to notice the days or weeks of my mother's tense conversations about my aunt's condition until Charlotte landed in the hospital for the last time.

We went to see her that night, lying so still and pale under the too-bright lights of an emergency room cubicle, where she was waiting to be admitted. I held my mother's hand, and she was crying. I was numb and too young to realize that this would be the last time I would see my aunt alive.

Charlotte never regained consciousness, so I never really had the chance to say goodbye. I kissed her cheek before we left that night. I remember how cool it felt, as well as so soft and velvety, even though she was an old woman.

I always wondered: what would Charlotte have done if she had been me, the night of my date, locked in the empty restaurant with Harry and Hans? I tried to imagine our conversation, perhaps sitting in one of those sticky, vinyl booths in Lloyd's café, where she and my mother had lunched so many Tuesday afternoons.

"So, Aunt Charlotte, I wore that outfit you helped me pick out last weekend. On a date," I'd begin. *"You know, the one with the navy-blue hat."*

"Oh, I do remember," she'd reply with a smirk. *"It was such a sassy look, the long coat with that sexy hat. Did you wear it kinda tilted to the side like I told you?"*

"I did. But it kinda got me in some trouble."

She would listen to the story of the entire evening, from Harry's stomping into our kitchen with his Frankenstein shoes to his promise to call the next time he was in town. I can almost see how her brow would wrinkle at some parts of the story, and how she would have giggled when I told her about Harry grabbing my hand and putting it *there*.

When I was all through, she would have leaned towards me across the table and lowered her voice so no one else could hear.

"Well," she'd begin, *"for one thing, I would have made sure I'd gotten at least one glass of wine out of the deal. You should have insisted—after all, the little turd was breaking the law just taking you into that restaurant when it was closed. I would have ordered a glass of the most expensive wine on their list, I would have."*

"But Aunt Charlotte," I'd say, *"what would you have done really? Wouldn't you have been scared?"*

She would reach across toward me then, clasping both of my hands into her wrinkled ones, her fingers adorned with two or three large-stoned rings, the neatly filed tips still painted a brilliant red. She'd squeeze my hands and smile into my eyes, mine the same luminous green as hers, just like she had so many times as I'd grown from a child into a young woman.

"You did well to get out of that situation, Frannie," she'd say softly. "I'm glad nothing bad happened, or your father would have killed both Harry and me. But please, don't blame the hat. There's nothing wrong with trying to attract a man's attention. You just had some bad luck. Harry was the wrong kind of guy. He was a creep." She'd pat my hands then and pull away, looking down into her lap, so I couldn't see what she was really saying with her eyes. But I'd hear her mumble,

"You can't help that you're so much like your mother."

Runway

After the Harry incident, I survived my teenage years and actually dared to date again—but not very much and chose my attire even more cautiously. Then fate stepped in, bringing my husband and me together. I was twenty and suddenly getting married. It all happened very fast, a quick decision, but one that's held up for over half of my life. And that's just so far.

We'd been married three years when my husband's job took us from New York to Florida. I was excited and anxious for this new life. Long winter coats and stylish hats were snazzy, but how glamorous was it to live in a subtropical climate, where bright colors and filmy fabrics defined the fashion world?

Florida was good for us. We had a lovely home in a small town; and over the next five years, I began my career in laboratory technology in the local hospital. Susie was five when her twin brothers came along. Clark had a great job teaching middle school and coaching basketball. There was never enough time or money, but we were deliriously happy; the perfect American family.

But something, for me, was still missing. I felt incomplete and inept in a very personal sense. I had regained an enviable figure, even after two pregnancies. But my sense of personal style, my body image, remained embryonic. I remained hidden under a uniform: scrubs for work, and "mom jeans" the rest of the time.

No matter how diligently I studied the fashion magazines, how relentlessly I shopped, or how carefully I chose my wardrobe, I never felt properly dressed. I was painfully self-conscious, and convinced that no matter what the occasion, I showed up either too casual or over- dressed.

My best friend Loraine, who had followed a different path those first years after high school, entered the business world as a fabulously wardrobed single girl. I had no reason to envy her, since I had what I'd always wanted—a loving husband, a home, healthy children. Yet every time I saw her on visits back north, I felt like she knew something I didn't. She always looked like she'd stepped off the pages of Cosmopolitan or Vogue. Loraine possessed what I still did not— confidence, poise, and comfort with her body image.

What I didn't know then was that my clothes were not the problem. My insecurities lie deeper, whether I draped them with a sundress or a designer suit. My deficiency was hidden way down underneath my skin.

I yearned for the same flare as I'd imagined my late Aunt Charlotte had clicking down the sidewalks of Madison Avenue in her heels, silk dresses, and matching hats. I decided I needed schooling on style. So after my kids started school and I was still young enough to reinvent my life, I applied to the International Academy of Design in Tampa. My husband, always the supportive angel, encouraged my whim, both emotionally and financially.

The day I received the letter from the Academy stands out as a high point in my life. After I'd ripped open the envelope and read that beautiful word—*accepted*—I laid down the wooden spoon I'd been using to stir the macaroni and cheese. I stepped around my toddler boys to pour myself a glass of cheap wine from the box in our fridge.

The twins giggled as they watched me perform a little happy dance. Susie, by then about eight years old, stomped into the kitchen and demanded, "What's everybody so happy about?"

My two years of training at the International Academy taught me how to sketch a design, drape cloth on a mannequin, and draft my own patterns. I discovered my penchant tended towards formal wear and bridal gowns, in particular. I guess somewhere deep inside, I'd always wanted to be Cinderella's fairy godmother.

Two long years of enduring the daily fifty-mile commute to downtown Tampa culminated on the runway at the Academy's Annual Fashion Show. The event happened at the glitzy downtown Tampa Sheraton. That night, I got a taste of the designer's life— backstage.

I never felt so small in my entire life. I'd been plucked out of Lilliput and dropped into the land of Gulliver's women. They may look svelte on the stage; but basically, up close and personal, fashion models are huge—most tower well over six feet. I top out at barely five foot four and felt like the mouse someone let in the back door.

It is true models are thin, some approaching emaciation. But females as tall as these, waltzing around in their size ten shoes, are imposing no matter how little they weigh. Their facial features are more extreme than what you could call beautiful, especially at close range. Those I met that night also seemed hardened by the grueling attributes of their profession.

One thing was for certain: I wouldn't have wanted to piss off any single one of them.

Our task as Academy graduates, i.e., "budding designers," was to outfit our assigned model, making sure every seam lay straight, and there were no bunches or bags anywhere. Students were required to provide everything, from the necessary undergarments to shoes and jewelry. The salesgirl at the shoe store raised an eyebrow and glanced down at my measly size seven loafers when I said I needed those satin-covered stilettos in a size ten.

Our model's glide down a glaringly lit runway was ever so brief. Everything had to be perfect. The show hall was filled; and although a good proportion of the seats had been reserved for the families of the graduates, the press was there as well: newspaper reporters, a few fashion magazine representatives, and a number of industry talent scouts. Open to the public—at a hundred bucks a seat—meant the promise of future clientele was very real. We had been instructed to bring business cards, the expensive, raised-letter kind. A table outside the entrance displayed our cards and other marketing media.

We didn't meet our models until thirty minutes before the show. In essence, our task had been to create a perfectly fitted, custom-designed garment for someone we'd never met. Luck had lots to do with our presentation that night. We were told to produce our designs in a standard size eight (which, in comparison with the ready-to-wear version of this size, was fairly generous) and bring all accessories and size ten shoes. Our instructors also advised we carry a needle, matching thread, and enough straight pins to tuck up a hem or pinch in a baggy seam.

There were more than ninety garments scheduled for debut that night and not more than a dozen models. Each leggy lovely spent less than sixty seconds on the runway and overlapped—there were never fewer than three models on the runway at any given moment. Logistically, that meant each fledgling designer backstage had less than three minutes to undress their model, re-outfit her, and send her back out to flaunt his or her signature design—perfectly.

Our entire future depended upon the outcome of less than four minutes.

Backstage was a scene out of a comedy review. Six or seven towering women frantically dropped clothing around their ankles—bras flying through the air, shoes bouncing off the partitions and patterned hose floating across the aisle like streamers. A lot of screaming—well, not really screaming—but frenzied whispering among the several dozen Lilliputian designers who ran around with bunched brow lines and pins in their mouths.

It was a magical night. My two wedding gowns were well-received, although definitely departed from the white classics. One, a basically traditional Victorian design, I'd re-envisioned in caramel beige taffeta. The other was white satin, but sported peach gussets that reached all the way from hem to hip. The portrait collar was puff-quilted and hand-encrusted with sequins and pearls.

What made me want to recreate the white wedding gown in a very non-traditional way? I know my own sense of creativity had something to do with it. The Academy definitely encouraged us to push the limits of convention. Perhaps, subconsciously, I was challenging a concept.

Reviews of the Academy's fashion show hit the Tampa newspapers the very next day. I was disappointed. Their descriptions were generic; and although they raved about the "exciting talent of the International Academy's graduating class," no specific mention was made of my gowns. None of that mattered, though, when my telephone rang just a few days later. A society lady from Carrollwood had attended the affair. Her daughter was newly engaged, and she'd chosen me to design the gown.

The appointment was for two p.m. at the client's home in a ritzier section of north Tampa. My mind buzzed like a pinwheel, as I made the hour-long journey, and my stomach felt like it was filled with swamp sludge. I knew this was the culmination of everything I'd been working so hard for over the past two years.

But this was different from coming up with a unique design in my own sewing room, where no one's tastes mattered but my own. Now, I would have someone else's imagination to consider. A paying customer. And it wasn't just any dress I was creating. Theoretically, a wedding gown is that one important dress worn only one day in a prospective bride's life. My window for success opened wider than my sixty seconds on the runway, but not by much.

I was terrified.

When I pulled into the driveway, I took a deep breath, carefully unloaded my sketch book and portfolio from the trunk of my car and made my way up to the peach-colored front door. It was the same hue as the gussets in my fashion show creation and contrasted beautifully with the fronds of the exotic palms and ferns bowing gracefully over the slate walk. I clearly remember the doorbell, encircled by an illuminated ring. Pressing that button seemed one of the most important actions I'd performed in my entire life.

The bride's mother greeted me. I followed her through a cloistered entryway that gave way to a scene straight out of Home & Garden: tumbled stone-tiled floors and cleverly placed recessed lighting. The mood screamed posh. Watercolors and gilt-framed oils graced the walls in strategic locations above classically elegant furniture. Mrs. Pampano invited me into their formal dining room and offered me a glass of iced tea.

"Alexis will be down in just a minute," she said. "Today was her spa day, and her masseuse was running a little behind schedule."

I smiled but said nothing. I spread my portfolio on the transparent table top, catching sight as I did of my slightly worn black loafers through the glass. I panicked. I hadn't dressed properly—certainly not like a designer. I didn't have time to worry long because moments later Alexis appeared through the archway down the other end of the room.

She was a lovely girl, tall and slender with a deep olive complexion. Her head was capped with soft black curls; and when she smiled, her eyes invited me right in. As she clasped my hand, she gushed, "So you're the artist who's going to make my dream gown a reality?"

My heart somersaulted in my chest, but I stood up a little taller, smiled back, and said, "That's certainly my intention."

Over the next hour, we transformed the massive dining table into a designer's drafting bench. Alexis had been dreaming up this gown of hers for quite some time. She'd collected a dozen or more dog-eared copies of bridal magazines, some dating back five years. One by one, she flipped them open and fanned the pages in front of me while her mother explained apologetically, "She's has been a fan of bridal magazines since she was just a little girl."

"This is my favorite neckline," Alexis began, pointing to a photo from *Modern Bride*, which was far from modern anymore. "And I absolutely love this bodice. I definitely want a cathedral train. I always thought I wanted long sleeves, but our wedding is in June. Yet I definitely don't want sleeveless. What are your recommendations?"

The dauntingly impossible task revealed glimmers of hope. Alexis made the process easier than I imagined. Although she asked me to create a unique gown for her, in reality, she had already designed the gown herself. Her collection of photographs of different gowns comprised pieces of a puzzle. All I had to do was connect them into one dress.

I picked up my charcoal pencil and began to sketch. Sketching is a first semester course at the Academy. If you can't create a visual image of your idea, it's impossible to sell. Fortunately, I was pretty good at it. I'd sailed through Sketching 101 with ease.

But that day, I felt like a preschooler with a stubby crayon. I scowled down at the oversized pad. I glanced repeatedly at all the glossy photos spread out on the table, before tentatively scratching the next line of charcoal on the page. I tried to ignore the silence, and how both women were staring at me. The room seemed to be getting warmer by the minute. I took care to keep my clammy forearm off the page as I sketched, so I didn't smear the soft pencil lines. It was a very long twenty minutes, but finally it was done.

"There." I sat back, pushed the sketch pad across the table and lifted my glass of tea, the only thing in the room sweatier than I was. "Is this what you had in mind?"

Their reaction was a small miracle. Mom's face crumpled into tears as her daughter's lit up with joy.

"Yes! Oh my God, yes, that's it! I can't believe you can do that!"

A silent thought ran through my brain: I only hope to God I can.

Over the next six months, Alexis and her mom came to my studio for her multiple fittings. These ladies were, I was to discover, dream clients. The bride knew exactly what she wanted, and her mother was gracious enough to honor her decisions. The first stage of fitting consists of a mere muslin shell, no skirt and no sleeves, not a bit of lace or a pearl in sight. But the shell allowed me to make all the crucial adjustments to the pattern I'd drafted before laying a set of shears to the imported Alencon lace that cost almost a hundred dollars a yard.

I tried to preface each of Alexis' appointments with a detailed description of the process. But by her third fitting, I could see disappointment in those dark eyes. It's hard for a layman to imagine what a finished bridal gown is going to look like from just scraps of fabric and lace, a paper sketch, and a facsimile fashioned of crude cotton.

"Don't worry," I reassured her. "The next time you see me, you will be trying on a real wedding gown."

And she did. I had her gown completely assembled except for some finishing beadwork and the zipper; and upon her arrival, it was displayed in all its magnificence on a padded dress form. I placed the figure in front of the wall of mirrors, so a first glance provided not only a front view, but the back as well, where I'd neatly pinned the closure, so you couldn't even tell the zipper was missing.

The gown was simple, classic, but magnificent. A bodice entirely covered with French re-embroidered lace was literally encrusted with tiny natural pearls. The color was champagne, a hue that enhanced Alexis' lovely olive complexion. The portrait neckline and short cap sleeves were edged with the lace's inherent scallop. A full, silk taffeta skirt was patched with more lace and pearls, and the train lengthened gracefully behind the gown for a full nine feet.

Again, as on that first day, Alexis's eyes glimmered with excitement while her mother's dissolved in tears.

Three months later, I received a formal invitation to Alexis' wedding. It was to be held in a modern church in North Tampa, with the reception scheduled for a five- star restaurant on the rooftop of the Marriott overlooking Tampa Bay. The wedding was six o'clock on a Saturday: formal attire recommended. It was then I realized that my work was not yet complete. Alexis' creation of pearls and lace would not be the only thing on display.

What on earth was I going to wear?

I knew it had to be spectacular, but not enough to draw attention away from the bride. I knew it had to be original, since it would be yet another opportunity to display my talents. And I knew, above all else, I had to look the part of the designer.

As the organ music began and we all rose to our feet, I was more nervous than the bride. I had created not only the bride's gown, but her headpiece and veil, as well as the pink satin sheath dresses wrapping the variably- sized torsos of the four bridesmaids and maid of honor. The fashion success of the entire female portion of the wedding party was my responsibility.

If a zipper popped or a hem didn't hang quite straight, it would be my fault. The imperfections would be forever recorded on film, on video, and indelibly in multiple memories. It would be a disaster from which I could never recover. I got lightheaded and dizzy halfway through the ceremony when I realized that I kept forgetting to breathe.

But no disasters befell my first big design debut. As the sun dipped low over Tampa Bay, I made my way to the Marriott and stepped into the elevator to be lifted to the twenty-second floor. When those doors slid open, I couldn't believe my eyes.

My charcoal sketch of Alexis' gown, the one I'd made the very first day, perched on an easel. It was framed in ornate gold and flanked by sprays of orchids and baby's breath. I remembered Mrs. Pampano asking for the original drawing at the final fitting, when it was obvious I no longer needed it as a guide. She had asked me to sign it. I never dreamed that humble pencil sketch would find its way to the rooftop.

I could not have imagined a more euphoric event. The bride's mother led me around by the elbow, introducing me to her guests as "Alexis's designer." And as I passed the wall of mirrors near the elevator, I knew I'd succeeded in looking the part. I found the fabric for the dress I designed for myself in an artsy, little cloth shop downtown. The imported silk was a bright floral, with pinks and ivory contrasting against an ebony background. I fashioned the cloth into a fitted and elegant sheath, unique but not straying far from a classic silhouette.

At the last minute, with Aunt Charlotte's words spurring me from memory, I chose a hat.

It was a broad-brimmed straw, dyed shiny jet black. I wrapped the crown with cherry ribbon and tacked a cluster of fresh ivory roses on one side. I was the only one at the wedding who wore a hat. But then, I was the only designer.

Although my stint as bridal designer was short-lived, I left a small legacy. Over the next five years, I outfitted about a dozen weddings in all, including several within our family. My brother's wife walked down the aisle in a satin gown heavy with pearls and iridescent sequins that twinkled like a galaxy of stars. My husband's brother got married about a year later. His wife's gown was elegant in its simplicity, swathing her in yards of taffeta the color of vanilla ice cream.

Custom clothing design is a tough business, and my experience with Alexis, I was to discover, was unusual at best. The bridal venue is the most difficult because the event is so important, and the clients so highly charged with emotion. I found the brides were not usually the problem; it was the mothers. Moms have their own mental image of their daughter's gown, one usually differing from the bride's. More than one mother- daughter bickering session ended in a full-blown screaming match in my studio.

My part in these dramas was precarious; since although I had to please both women, Mom was usually the one with the checkbook.

And then there was the size issue. Most brides plan far in advance and up to a year can elapse between that first measuring session and the wedding day. Stress has differing effects on different people: some lose weight; some gain it. I found myself worrying more about my clients' eating habits than my own. More than once, I improvised in the wee hours the night before a wedding, adding a three-inch gusset on a waistline or tucking that much away in a cleverly concealed pleat. The stress level of my chosen profession, backlit with the anxieties of managing a home and a family, approached the absurd.

I spent countless hours squinting through a magnifying glass, hand stitching a zipper or invisibly securing microscopic beads to lace. I grew weary of sleepless nights, worrying about the next day's fitting appointment. I finally gave up my whim of bridal designer. I decided that the wonderful world of fashion was much more fun enjoyed as a spectator sport.

But I'd accomplished my goal. I convincingly wore the hat of fashion designer. I challenged one of society's conventions, albeit in a small way, by willfully altering the niveous purity of the wedding gown. I know my creations never graced the cover of Bride's

Magazine or any fashion rag for that matter. But my education in fashion taught me it was okay to buck the trends, to express my unique personality rather than to reflect some mass-marketed ideal. I had affronted tradition and in the process, gained confidence to exhibit my own personal style.

Sadly, by this time in my life, my mother and I had grown apart. I was approaching thirty, had a full-time job, a rambunctious family, and pursued yet still another dream. Physical distance was not to blame. My parents had followed us south after Dad retired, and they lived only a few miles away. The problem was I was living a life neither of my parents could understand nor approve of. I had matured into a woman whose life was not the image of my mother's.

My roles of wife and mother were not my full-time occupations. I was, selfishly in their eyes, pursuing dreams of my own.

My parents did attend the fashion show when I graduated from the Academy. But instead of accolades for my unique and colorful interpretations of the traditional wedding gown, they responded with stilted comments under raised eyebrows. It was almost as though, by drifting away from the purity of the white wedding gown, I'd committed a sacrilege.

Somehow, I knew if Charlotte had been there, she would have been proud.

Powder Pink

We buried my mother when my daughter was seventeen. Mom died of throat cancer. She'd never had her tonsils removed; and after suffering for four months with a sore throat that wouldn't go away, the tumor had spread into her sinuses and invaded her jawbone. Just one year after the diagnosis, Mom passed away.

Every second of those horrific days brands my memory. The months of radiation, and the burns she suffered from her chin to her breasts; the day she asked me to trim her hair, and I stood over her weeping as most of the strands fell loose from her scalp, clinging to the comb as I worked; watching her previous, too-hefty figure wither to a frail shadow of the person she once was. I worked in the pathology lab where her biopsy was processed.

I was the one sitting across from the pathologist who looked at the slide under the microscope. When dear Dr. Jonas looked up at me, there were tears in his eyes. We both knew Mom was dying. These memories I have, for the most part, buried somewhere inside a pain-proof vault where they can no longer wake me in the middle of the night.

The aftermath, however, somehow won't fit into that coffer.

At the funeral home, they ushered us into a suite with heavy, dark furniture and elaborate arrangements of plants. The flowers and ferns were living, not silk. I found this odd, discomforting since the room had no windows. My oldest brother wheeled in our father, whose already sunken visage seemed somehow even more deflated. I took my place along with my brothers, hands folded, heads bowed, around a highly polished table.

The only way I maintained composure was to focus on the physical details: a thick gloss of shellac covering dark wood of a surface that felt sticky under my forearms, the sweet-sour scent of bright pink carnations hanging in stagnant air, a subdued glow from shell- shaped wall sconces against two-toned beige, paisley wallpaper.

Paisley, I thought. Great. My father hated paisley.

I pretended I was an extra in a scene from The Godfather. Accompanied by three tall dark men in darker suits and a graying patriarch slumped in a wheelchair, the family was about to make enduring decisions around this table. The remainder of my own, nuclear family, my husband and daughter, hung back, seated at the perimeter of the room. Crouched between my two older brothers, I felt very small.

I was the only daughter.

But by that time, I had a daughter of my own, who was old enough and had a mind enough of her own to wait only a moment before pulling her chair up right behind me. The macabre process began, dreamlike and surreal. I'd never arranged for anyone's funeral before.

The sensation of Susie's fingers gripping my left elbow seemed my only tether from drowning.

All I kept thinking was, How unfair. How could anyone put a price on what would be my mother's final resting place? My family had never been well-to-do, creeping along from one monthly check to the next. The life insurance policy was cashed in long ago to pay for the cost of living: a new TV when the old one's tubes burned out; decking and a ramp for the new front porch, added when my father became part of his wheelchair; and the ever-climbing premium for the Medicare Gap insurance. Our decision to insist her casket be "pretty" seemed frivolous, especially considering how simply my mother had lived. But we all felt better that it was. We chose a steel box with shiny gunmetal blue on the outside, powder blue satin within. Blue, after all, was her favorite color.

The funeral director was a talented actor. He spoke as though he'd personally known my mother. We all knew he'd never seen Mom breathing.

"I will need one of you to bring the clothing that Ruth will wear."

Ruth, I thought? Really? Even my father seldom called her that. In fact, I almost never heard my father address my mother by her given name. It was always simply "Hon." She didn't have friends close enough to address her that way. Only Aunt Charlotte called her "Ruth." More often, "Ruthie."

None of us had considered her burial outfit until that meeting. Of course, Mom would have to be dressed up, look nice—at least as nice as one could look when dead. My brothers exchanged nervous glances, while Daddy's head hung forward listlessly. He was, though, the patriarch. He had to make the decisions. After a pause, the funeral director repeated his request, more pointedly this time.

"What will your wife wear, Mr. Del Negro?"

My mother had never been a fashion queen. Her faded housecoats and polyester tunics certainly wouldn't do for this occasion. She hadn't owned a "nice" dress since my younger brother's wedding some years back and that had been passed along to charity long ago.

Cliché, perhaps, but a sad truth: here had arrived her final, big moment, and Mom truly didn't have a thing to wear.

My brothers stared down at their hands, fidgeting. The moment began to stretch and warp, and the air in the windowless room settled thick on the table. I struggled to draw each breath, glancing around the room, then into my lap, making every effort to avoid eye contact with my brothers. But I could sense the inevitable. Slowly, one by one, each of them decided. When I glanced up, they were all staring at me.

Mom needed a pretty dress to be buried in. Fashion was a female task. There would have to be one last shopping excursion.

Gulfview was the nearest mall. It had been, once upon a life, a mother-daughter playground, a family tradition for birthdays and holidays, and a place where the annual Christmas shopping would commence.

Sometimes all three of us would go. Other times, it was just Mom and me. The mall had earned a reputation for us, a place of laughter and girl talk, window shopping and dreaming. Today would be different. There would be no window shopping today. My daughter and I were there to make a purchase.

Macy's entrance was always wide and inviting, but today the lights were too bright, and the floor too shiny. Every chrome rack of garments looked eerily the same; dresses lined up neatly on cushioned hangers. The mannequins stared. I'd never noticed before how artificially the displays were staged. It seemed, morosely, a perfect rehearsal for us. How much different is a funeral?

The blonde salesclerk was cheerful and almost too friendly. We explained our mission in generic terms: to pick out the perfect dress for a very special occasion, for my mom, for Susie's Grandma.

"What size does your mother wear?"

We didn't tell her that the woman we were shopping for was dead. The big event was a funeral. The dress would be worn until it disintegrated into dust along with its wearer.

Susie kept her eyes on the racks, busily snapping through the hangers.

"What size, Mama?"

My daughter repeated herself when I didn't respond, her tone clipped the second time. It was a good question, and I hesitated because I truly didn't know the answer. My mother had struggled with her weight ever since I could remember. I knew this dress would be a much smaller size than she'd ever worn.

Ironically, Mom died enviably thin—at least in accordance with current fashion standards. The tumor, the radiation, and the poisons they'd pumped into her body had sheared off the pounds motherhood and maturity had heaped on. As I slid metal hooks along an icy steel bar, I recalled earlier shopping ventures and heard my mother's voice through my pain.

"I know you can't believe it to look at me now, but my wedding dress was a size ten. A perfect ten."

That was before the diagnosis, before the treatments began.

What's considered in vogue to be buried in? My mother didn't dress up often and even then, preferred the simple and basic. She never wanted to draw attention to herself. The dresses there were too flashy, too sexy, or too red—cocktail wear. Others were too *funeral*—like something to be worn *to* a funeral, but by those still living.

I thought of my late Aunt Charlotte. I wondered now, all these years later, who had picked out her burial dress. I didn't even remember what she'd worn. I'm sure it wasn't flashy enough for her liking, not unless there'd been a matching hat. On record, she didn't have a daughter to pick out her clothes for this, the last big outing.

Or did she?

I remember little about the preparations for Aunt Charlotte's funeral, mostly because I was, emotionally, not old enough. I was too immature to support my mother in her grief. Even though I was almost the same age as Susie was when my Mom passed away. Surely, Mom had decided what Aunt Charlotte would wear for her last big gig. I am ashamed now that not only do I not remember what my aunt wore— is still wearing—but I offered my mother no assistance in helping make that choice.

Now, I was in my mother's place, feeling what she must have felt in those tortuous days before the coffin lid was closed and latched. Standing under the too- bright lights of Macy's, making a decision that somehow seemed to be the most important choice I would make in my entire life.

I remember wandering, almost frantically, through endless racks of satin and sequins and lace, hoping my heart would lead me in the right direction. Finally, I noticed a display set apart from the others, surrounded by a mirrored alcove. All the dresses on the circular rack were identical, some pink and some blue. Sparkly organza overlaying taffeta, a simple design, with just enough lace and beads. The gown had long sleeves and a high neckline. Perfect. So much the better to cover needle bruises and radiation burns.

Susie followed, silent until then, never less than an arm's reach from my side.

"I think this one is perfect, Mama. Which color?" Susie leaned in close to keep our consultation hushed. The sales clerk had lost interest in us, wandering off to accost another customer.

"It has to be the blue. You know her favorite color was blue," I whispered.

"I know, Mom, but the casket lining is light blue. Blues can be tricky—it's not like we have a swatch or anything to make sure the colors don't clash."

How horrible, I thought. What a travesty to be caught wearing two shades of blue that don't go well together—not just for one occasion, but for the rest of time. How awful when all those mourners, whom I was certain would notice immediately, whispered, "Oh! Those colors just don't look well together at all!"

But maybe Susie was right. Still, the decision made me feel as if I were betraying my mother one last time. As a child, Mom and I had shared our favorite color as blue. As I'd matured, I'd come to prefer pink.

"What size, Mama?" Susie pressed. "What did she used to wear?"

"A twelve or fourteen, but that wouldn't fit her now.

She lost so much weight . . . "

"How about this one? A size ten?" Susie snatched the hanger off the rack and laid the dress across her forearm.

"It still looks way too big. She was down under a hundred pounds, Susie." My throat began to seize with pain.

My daughter turned to face the salesgirl, hovering at a respectful distance. Susie's words hissed through a rigid set of her lips.

"What's the smallest size this one comes in? In the pink?"

It was a size four.

As the clerk rang up the purchase, she said chattily, "They call this color powder pink. It's so elegant...some pinks can be overwhelming. But this one is elegant. Elegant without being gaudy."

Elegant, but not too gaudy. Just like my mother.

I was proud. I'd held my composure and hadn't made a scene. I hadn't broken down and embarrassed my teenage daughter in the store where she came to buy her designer jeans and Estee Lauder lipsticks.

The smiling clerk casually slipped a white, plastic dress bag over the gown and passed the cold, metal hook into my hand. I was fine. Then she added, "I'll bet your mother will love it."

That did it.

Mom's dresses had mostly come from discount stores or thrift shops. Many she'd fashioned on her own sewing machine. Her wedding dress wasn't even a proper gown, but a simple, navy blue linen suit she'd found on a clearance rack at Filene's basement in a frugal past I could only imagine. I was fairly certain that all of Mom's dresses came home in a plain sack, never draped in plastic on a cushioned hanger like this one. When the shrouded gown was passed into my hand, reality punched me in the gut. This was the fanciest dress my mother would ever own.

The air around me grew thick, like hot gelatin in a bowl when ice cubes are stirred into it. I became acutely aware of strange women all around me, dressed in designer sweaters, their heavy suede jackets draped carefully over multi-bangled wrists. The air grew thicker. Its weight hung over me, pressing my arm lower, lower, until the draped hem of pink organza brushed the shiny aisle floor.

But like a buoy, there was a hand under my left elbow. Strong fingers gently lifted my arm to keep the hem clear of the floor. My eyes flashed to my daughter's, my gaze a silent scream. Raising one eyebrow, Susie spoke—her words firm, bold, and just a little too loud.

"Mom, do you need to find a ladies' room, or do you just want to walk out of here?"

As she drove us home, I studied Susie's profile, softly illuminated in the glow of the dashboard lights. I hadn't noticed until then how high cheekbones had emerged from a round face, how a dimpled chin had become chiseled. Her pursed lips seemed fuller, mature, almost sensual.

Susie was barely eighteen. Emotional support, until then, had always been my job.

Where had this creature come from? That's what I remembered thinking. Certainly, her maturity, this strength and boldness, hadn't come from me. Susie was as close—in some ways, perhaps even closer—to my mother than I had been. It was not lack of grief that gave my daughter this solid base, this ability to take the reins from me, hold me up, and carry me on through those next horrific days.

My mother obviously passed on knowledge and taught me how to raise a kind and caring daughter. But that strength of will and spirit? Those were qualities I could not possibly have given Susie. They had come from somewhere farther down the trunk of the family tree.

Portrait

My mother's death left my father alone, for the first time in the over fifty years they'd been married. By then, he was in a wheelchair, a condition he never completely accepted. My younger brother, Frank, and I were the only two children who lived near enough at the time to see to his care. We both also worked full time and were raising families.

In the aftermath of Mom's death, we were quite proud of my dad. This man had never cooked a meal or washed a load of laundry in his life, yet he rallied to the challenge. He learned to take care of himself quite well, at least physically. Frank and I took turns visiting: taking him out to dinner, grocery shopping, and including him in family gatherings. But Daddy was less than half-whole without Mom. After three years, even though his health wasn't all that bad, he just gave up living.

We laid Daddy to rest beside Mom in March of 2001, in a lovely, serene spot of the Veterans Cemetery in Webster, Florida.

Although Frank and I had banded together to help Mom and Dad in those final years, my younger brother and I were never close. In age, we were only two years apart; and as kids, we had vied for premium status; he was the baby, but I was the only daughter. Competition ensured we never got along well. So, when his name popped up in my e-mail inbox one night a few years after Daddy died, I fought trepidation and clicked open the link.

Hey Fran, I was just thinking about that old picture we had of our grandmother. You know—the one where's she's wearing a hat. Do you know whatever happened to it?

The portrait of the woman in a cloche hat sat on the mantle in my home office. I smiled over my shoulder towards the original leather-bound frame. Then I typed back,

Yeah, I do. I'm looking at her right now. She watches over me as I write.

Branded into memory, the photo was a staple on my mother's bureau ever since I could remember. Nestled amid clusters of oddly shaped bottles of Avon perfume, spot lit by a boudoir lamp with a dusty, fluted shade, it was the bust portrait of a proud-looking young woman. An original black and white image had been hand- tinted in shades of green. Her eyes were the same luminous hue as the trim on her collar. She wore a brimless helmet style hat, the cloche, a popular classic in the 1920s. Time and again, Mom referred to the portrait as one of her mother. It was, she stressed time and again, the only one she had.

When young, one takes many things for granted. A dusty portrait of a lady in a weird hat from another era meant nothing to any of us kids. Until Frank's e-mail that day, the portrait was never mentioned. It was just another *thing*—a physical fragment of what had once been the life of a vital human being.

But *things* were all that were left after Mom passed away, and my father clung to them like a life raft. After the funeral, Dad allowed nothing of hers to be moved. He scolded anyone who touched the Tupperware container in the center of the kitchen table. The plastic oval cradled Mom's last work-in-progress. She loved to crochet. The needlework, along with everything else defining her, remained frozen in place until three years after her death when Dad finally joined her. Not long after, Frank and I began the gruesome process of cleaning out their crumbling old doublewide trailer before it was hauled away.

Those days of sorting and sifting were tortuous. Memory jogs can be bittersweet, but most were sheer agony. After Dad's funeral, everything happened too fast. When he died, it was like losing both of them at once. To walk through the house, you would never know she'd been gone before him, inflating the macabre chore exponentially.

My parents were pack rats. They never threw anything away. As a result, their modest-sized, three-bedroom home held enough miscellaneous "stuff" to supply a full-blown flea market. My mother loved yard sales, and my father collected a variety of trinkets. Although these things were now all that remained of them, it was impractical, impossible to keep them all. Frankie and I designated four piles in the center of the living room: the things I wanted, the things he wanted, the things going to Goodwill, and the things nobody would want—the trash heap.

A distinct aura hung in their bedroom, a feeling Mom had just run out to the store and would return any minute. The heels of her worn pink terry scuffs peeked out from under her side of the bed. Her embroidered yellow housecoat hung from the back of the door, right where she'd last left it. It still smelled like her. The cloisonné earrings she'd worn to her last oncology appointment—the last time she went out when she still cared how she looked—remained side by side atop her pink padded jewelry box. And the portrait of her mother still perched, where it always had, on the end of her bureau.

My father's effects were less appealing. An overfilled amber ashtray overwhelmed his nightstand. A lidded plastic denture cup dominated the bathroom counter. His black canvas loafers were all but threadbare, still tucked side-by-side under his chair.

But nothing spoke as distinctly about my father as his shrine. His bureau served as stage for a divine assembly—a half-dozen faded, cracked figurines of Jesus, Mary, St. Joseph, St. Francis, along with several other saints neither Frankie nor I could confidently identify. The shrine on Dad's dresser was as much a part of childhood memory for us as the portrait on Mom's bureau. I can still see my Dad in his baggy Dickies and a stretched-out tee shirt, making the sign of the cross every time he passed his dresser. Sometimes he'd stop, kiss the end of a bony finger, and touch it to the head of Jesus or Mary.

The ceramic figures were sizable, some over a foot high. To call them vintage was an understatement. The details of St. Joseph's eyes and mouth had worn almost completely away, and the brown paint on St. Francis's robe was flaking into a pile around his sandaled feet. Chipped off somewhere in the long years, Mary was missing part of one hand yet still securely clutched the baby Jesus. They displayed a sad pageant. But their presence in a house where nobody lived anymore created an interesting dilemma for my brother and me. What does one do with timeworn religious statues?

"Do you want any of these?" I had the learned reverence for the saints, my father's ritual branded into memory. I knew Daddy had worshiped these things; but to be honest, the statues always gave me the creeps. Frankie chuckled.

"Naw, I don't think I could bring these into my house. The kids would have nightmares."

"Well, I know I don't want 'em," I mumbled, almost ashamed. The stillness in the house was palpable, lacking the drone of the television in the living room, one my father hadn't turned off since the day Mom died. It was early spring, but the relentless Florida sun was already heating up the dank air, creating a light show on the dust particles floating in the air around the statues. It lent them an eerie halo.

I took a deep breath and huffed into the silence. "Well, what do we do with them? Goodwill?"

Frank glared at me, scowling as he shook his head. "That's a sacrilege," he snapped. "That's worse than throwing them away."

"We can't trash them." I plopped down on the end of my parents' bed, the pastel-patched quilt still rumpled from the last time Daddy had climbed out. It had been barely weeks ago. Frankie and I sat in silence for a few moments, struggling with the still-fresh wounds of loss. We stared at the collection of statues, a time-ravaged crèche.

My brother suggested a practical approach. "We could put them on eBay. I'll bet somebody collects this kind of stuff."

"You can't auction them off on the Internet. Daddy would turn over in his grave."

"You're right. We can't do that." My brother was scratching his head. "I wonder if the church would want them."

I raised my eyebrows. "Do you want to offer these to the church? I think they might be insulted."

Frankie agreed with a nod and a hmm, then added, "Fran, what are we going to do with them?"

An hour later, my brother and I held a ceremony in the front yard of my parents' house. Frank wielded a shovel, and I the casket; a hard-sided, square cosmetic case, one my mother used to carry her makeup the few times they had travelled. Inside the box, nestled close together for all eternity, lay my father's timeworn collection of religious statues. We laid them to rest under the ground on the last property where my parents lived, in a little circular space bordered by the driveway. The spot was peaceful, shaded by young oaks. Frank and I bowed our heads and said a little prayer.

The property stayed in our family for another three years or so before it was sold. I always wonder if the new owners chose the spot for a shade garden. Hopefully, they didn't dig too deep. If they unearthed the casket, I wonder what they would think. Would they consider the find an omen of some kind? If so, good or bad? I can assure you, if it was blue iris they were planting, the omen was good. My mother loved blue iris.

Somewhere in those horrendous days of dismantling every last earthly trace of our parents, the portrait of my grandmother came up for grabs.

I grabbed it.

***

A few weeks after we'd finished dismantling my parents' household, I carried the portrait, carefully sandwiched in its leather-bound folder, with me to work. The Veterinary School Campus of Tufts University had a wonderful media services department. Andy ran the place.

"Andy, I need your professional opinion on something."

It was early on a Monday morning—way too early, evidently, because my friend rolled his eyes toward the ceiling and snapped back, "Oh, like I'm qualified to give you a professional opinion on anything."

"Come on, Andy, you're a photographer. Can you look at this picture and tell me the vintage?"

I handed him the leather-bound folder holding the portrait of my grandmother. Just the night before, I'd slid the image out from behind its protective film to check for a date or identifying mark on the back. The paper was thick and stiff, the back yellowed and splotched with a few pale brown stains. Nothing else.

Andy was now searching for clues in the same way. He flipped the crisp paper over, rubbing it between two fingers. Cocking his head, his brows drew together. Then he shot a glance up at me.

"This is not an original. This is a picture of a picture," he stated as if I should know this was obvious. "Look here, you can see how the original image had worn and frayed edges. There's also this fold line across the top." He pointed to the pale white line slicing through the woman's green-tinted right eye. Then he flipped the print over and examined the back closely. "The crack was on the original. There is no crack in this paper."

"Can you tell how old it is?"

"I don't know much about old photographs." He was staring at the image, brows raised. "Who is this, anyway?"

100

I took the print from him and was carefully sliding it back into its sleeve. "I've been told it's my grandmother."

"Your grandmother, huh? She looks very young here."

Andy took the folder from me and studied the image again. He shook his head and shrugged.

"I have no idea how old this print is, but I can tell you the original portrait looks to be 1920s vintage. They did a lot of hand-tinting back then. And this young woman is dressed like a flapper."

***

Mommy, who is the lady in the picture on your dresser?

It's a portrait of my mother. It's the only one I have.

What was her name?

Wilhelmina. But she hated her name. She went by Minnie. Minnie Winniett.

The silent, mysterious portrait sat on the mantle in my office—having occupied some critical place in my writing space since the day I claimed it off my mother's bureau. This woman, my grandmother, wasn't sharing any secrets. I'd carried her along with me for eight years, to four different states. She'd remained eerily silent.

Suddenly, the photograph or print of a portrait or whatever medium the image was—wasn't enough. My maternal grandmother demanded I investigate further. My mother's tales could no longer recharge my imaginings of a woman who purportedly died over forty years before I was born.

I needed to know her. Know who and how she was.

I loved exploring history, and I was exploring my own. My search began with Mom's birth and baptismal certificates, documents I'd seen only briefly after she died. They surfaced during the after-the-fact formalities, part of the paperwork a suit behind a desk in some government office required. Apparently, you can't be declared dead unless there's proof you'd been born.

My younger brother, Frank, had held these documents in his

possession since the funeral. He lived in Florida. Thanks to computers and the Internet and scanners, and to my brother's gracious cooperation, copies soon appeared in my inbox.

The PDF of Mom's New York State Certificate and Record of Birth was permanently creased by decades-old folds that struggled in vain to obscure the hand-inscribed details. But it declared basic facts about my mother: Ruth Lillian Fisher came into this world on February 27, 1922. Her mother resided at 152 Fisk Ave., Winfield. Mother's Marriage Name . . . *Wilhelmina Fisher*. Mother's Name before Marriage . . . *Wilhelmina Steuer*, whose recorded age was thirty-nine at the time of birth. Father . . . *Peter J. Fisher*, age twenty-nine.

I studied the Census records online, becoming one of *Ancestry.com*'s most frequent visitors. I could locate no marriage record where Wilhelmina Steuer became Mrs. Peter J. Fisher. And examination of the dates of my mother's birth certificate revealed it had been issued almost two full weeks *after* she was born.

Inklings in my memory stirred. Echoes of her voice, haltingly answering questions I'd put to her as a child. Questions she'd been uncertain—and unwilling—to answer.

"I was born at home. In fact, my mother and father went down to the county office when I was already two weeks old to apply for my birth certificate."

Home, for Wilhelmina or Minnie Winniett in 1920, according to the 1920 Census records, was 228 Fisk Ave., Winfield, Queens, New York. She resided there with her young son George and her daughter Charlotte, then fifteen years old.

Yet the address on my mother's birth certificate was 122 Fisk Ave., Winfield.

Okay, so her parents weren't married. Had Minnie moved in with Peter Fisher in those two years between that census and my mother's birth? Entirely possible.

But other critical details didn't seem to match. In 1922, according to all previous census records on which she appears, Minnie Winniett would have been forty- four years old. Yet on my Mom's birth certificate, Minnie's age is recorded as thirty-nine. Peter Fisher was twenty-nine.

Was Grandma a cougar? It was the Roaring Twenties, after all. Minnie Winniett could definitely have been one of those flappers, jumping up on the tables of the smoky, dark, illegal nightclubs doing the Charleston. Attracting the attention of a man fifteen years younger than she.

But birthing a baby at home in her mid-forties? And having two other young children at home to support? Minnie was not, it appeared, a woman of lavish means. Her occupation listed repeatedly on the census records of 1910, 1920, and 1930, was as "washerwoman" or "janitress."

The only other piece of hard evidence I had to trace was Mom's baptismal certificate, stating she was baptized on April 16, 1922. It appeared the clerk of the Church of B.V.M. Help of Christians had made a clerical error. Ruth Lillian Fischer—her last name bearing an additional, silent "c"—was the *"Child of Peter and Wilhelmina Winniett."*

Too many discrepancies stared back at me from what was left, the only fragments of my mother's—and by extension, my own—history. I had no choice. I had to dig further.

Wilhelmina . . . "Minnie"? Or Charlotte?

Lost in Time

Most children trust their parents, particularly when very young. An innocent, youthful mind absorbs truths from their parents as gospel. My mother said the portrait that sat on her bureau was of my grandmother. I never had any reason to doubt her. The story, along with that visual image, made my grandmother real in my world, though I'd been told she died a quarter century before I was born.

I knew so much less about my grandfather. I had no photograph, and the story my mother parroted was cryptic and always identical, as though she diligently memorized it. It was clear to me as an adult, though it had not been when I was a child: Mom had no memory of her father to share.

Your grandfather's name was Peter Fisher—you know, like "fisherman." He was a sailor. He died when I was just a baby. I never knew him.

***

Ancestry.com is a wonderful tool, though tricky to navigate at first. It is easy to get lost in their labyrinth of hints and clues, a maze that sometimes ends up wasting time without yielding any useful information. I'm not very savvy with computer software anyway. I'd already spent countless hours hopelessly lost in the website's caverns. But before I'd been searching a common name. Fisher, for which there were countless records. With this new spelling, the lists, though still pages deep, loomed less threatening.

One rainy Saturday, I was into my second hour of clicking and bumping into walls. Ready to call it quits and pour myself a glass of conciliatory chardonnay, I clicked on one last link. A window popped open framing a draft card.

The PDF was badly Xeroxed but still legible, dated 1918. The first discrepancy that jumped out at me was the fact that the name printed on the top of the card, Peter J. Fisher, didn't match the signature at the bottom. The loopy, quivery signature read Peter J. Fischer. There was the "c."

I was so excited, my hands started to shake, and I kept blinking at the screen, certain my eyes were deceiving me. Grabbing my drugstore readers and leaning closer to the screen, I scanned the address. 152 Fisk Ave., Maspeth, Queens. I'd uncovered an undeniable link. This Mr. Fisher, or Fischer, resided at the same address as the one recorded on my mother's birth certificate.

This surely had to be my grandfather.

When frantic clicks on the "Print" icon failed to send the document to my printer, a strange sense of surrealism gripped me. Surely my imagination had taken control. I closed and reopened the window repeatedly, holding my breath each time. I was terrified the document would disappear, slip irretrievably into the past. Finally the electronics synced. My printer groaned and hummed as the document inched out in agonizingly slow increments. I had it. My own personal copy of the truth.

A draft card. If there was a draft card, there must be a military record. My grandfather was a soldier. The comforting thing about veterans' cemeteries is this: armed with a name properly spelled on a government document, you can find dead soldiers even if they never knew you.

Veterans' cemeteries all look alike. Not only are they full of dead people, but on these grounds, there exists a comforting uniformity.

The deceased here share a common bond, for many the only one. Yet all are given equal ground. The white marble grave markers are all shaped the same way. The headstones are identical except for the configuration of letters and numbers carved into their stony surfaces. For me, the National Cemetery on Long Island, New York suddenly held new significance. That was where my grandfather was buried.

I drove up to the computerized kiosk, perched like an ATM outside a small brick building. My copy of the draft card in hand, I scrolled down the long list of Fischers. Finally, the right one appeared. I scribbled down the section letter and grave number and set out across the cemetery.

He was buried near the perimeter, in the middle of a row conforming to the outer, curved iron fence. A balmy breeze fluttered the leaves of an elm shading a nearby patch of open lawn. I wondered how that worked; tree roots and burial chambers. Did the diggers alter a site location when they hit a tap root? Did the groping roots of a growing tree find their way into the concrete vaults?

Glancing around me, I realized that the dates etched into the gravestones in this section were at least fifty years old, some older. I gazed up at the tree, huge and full, its trunk many times bigger around than me. The elm was stately, old, and had probably stood watch over the diggers who dug my grandfather's grave and laid him to rest.

I stood there for a long time, numb, not knowing how or what to feel. In some childish, ignorant way, I'd felt coming here would answer the gnawing questions and fill the void. I had found my grandfather, but the discovery left me empty and confused. The crucial details, the documented facts I'd uncovered, didn't match the story my mother had embedded in my memory.

All my life I'd inscribed my "Mother's Maiden Name" on countless legal documents, from my driver's license to marriage license and beyond. I now had proof I'd been spelling it wrong. Thanks to government record and lines etched into marble, I also now know that Peter J. Fischer was not a sailor, as Mom had repeatedly claimed, but a Private First Class in the U.S. Army. Mr. Fischer died in Queens, New York, right around the corner from where my mother was born. In 1965.

Your grandfather's name was Peter Fisher—you know, like "fisherman." He was a sailor. He died when I was just a baby. I never knew him.

I now knew a different truth. By the time my grandfather passed away, my mother was in her forties. I was already eight years old. And this man, her father, my grandfather, lived just a few blocks away from where she was born and grew up. Yet she claimed she never knew him.

It appeared I might have uncovered a well-kept secret.

My fertile imagination began to create possible scenarios. I'd now fixed my grandparents in time and place, in a wild and fast-changing New York City in the 1920s. Thanks to my grandmother's portrait, my mental image of her was clear, right down to the color of her eyes and the decoration on her hat. To imagine my grandfather required a bit more creative license.

I knew Mr. Fischer was a young man when Mom was born, not yet thirty. Although impossible for me to guess what he looked like, not even the color of his eyes, I liked to believe they were blue, like my mother's. I envisioned him as a man of short stature, or just average perhaps, since Mom was barely over five feet tall. I wagered he was a looker in his day, since in this, my version of the story, he'd apparently attracted the attention of an older woman. Quite a bit older. Minnie was sixteen years his senior.

I imagined he caught her eye because he spoke to her with those pale eyes. Perhaps it was because he wore a uniform, arresting attention, commanding respect with a cocky stance, leaning on a pillar in the subway station on some busy Friday evening. Or it may have been at the bus stop, on some lonely afternoon in late June, when the scent of fresh-cut grass in the park blossomed summer into something much more promising. I wonder if it was she who approached him. Perhaps Minnie was returning from work, tired and lonely. She may have asked him to join her for a drink, since prohibition ruled those times. Women found it difficult to access speakeasies alone.

The bars were dark, smoky and crowded, and the two probably sat close in a back booth, as he offered to light her cigarette. She would have leaned in close to him, beckoning him unabashedly with expressive green eyes. Conversation, playful and bright, carried them from the pub's dim light to a more private place. She may have mesmerized him with her practiced charm. I'm guessing all she wanted was a good time. For him, it may have meant much more. Maybe not. In any event, I know they spent a night, or at least part of one, together. Alone.

All of the creative details live only in my imagination, but one certainty is this: nine months after one evening in Queens in the summer of 1921, a new life drew breath from the meeting of a young soldier and the woman in the portrait. Sadly, by the time the baby girl made her entrance into the world, all that remained for her to inherit from Mr. Fischer was his name.

Why?

It is now nearly a hundred years later. The young man in uniform is long dead, and the older woman in the cloche hat has been dead even longer. And the baby girl? She's dead, too. The brothers and the sisters, the aunts and the nieces and nephews—everyone who knew even one of the pair who marked a small history that night—are gone. Then there's me, a persistently curious granddaughter on whose mantel sits a portrait of a flapper.

I stood in the August sunshine in the middle of Long Island National Cemetery surrounded by a sea of identical marble markers set in uniformly comforting concentricity. I'd accomplished my goal. I'd found Granddad. But now more questions than could ever be answered haunted me. Anyone who might answer them, if they even would, was long dead.

I started with the facts I had in hand. An address.

152 Fisk Ave., Winfield, Queens.

Winfield. A Google maps search didn't locate the town. MapQuest couldn't find it either. I checked the spelling and tried again, but Winfield did not turn up on any New York State map. A broader Internet search yielded a webpage called, "The Lost City of Winfield." Lost city?

My mother's city of birth sat right at a crossroads for new railroad lines that, in the early 1900s, rapidly gridded the fast-growing borough of Queens. Somewhere in the shuffle of progress, Winfield became an early twentieth century Atlantis.

Since I didn't know anything about the history of New York City or any of its boroughs (even though I'd been born in one of them), I decided a quick study was in order.

Somehow, some way, I needed to find out more about the history behind the woman who was my mother.

"It occupies a territory that has passed through all the epochs of the American past." That's what I'd discovered in a historical essay on the borough of Queens. Created on November 1, 1683, it was one of the ten original counties of New York State. In the early 1900s, the construction of the Penn Tunnels under the East River suddenly linked her with the growing urban center of Manhattan. During the 1920s, the population of Queens ballooned 130 percent, expanding her into a popular suburb for the working people of Manhattan. The housing industry couldn't keep up. There simply weren't enough homes being built fast enough to accommodate the need. As a result, vast numbers of construction workers from outlying areas traveled into Queens. Suddenly, many strangers roamed about in what was once a quiet community.

In the midst of all this expansion sat Winfield, a community wearing a shroud from early on. The town's main employer at the turn of the 20th century was the

W.M. Raymond Manufacturing Company whose main product was metal coffins. Could this have been the "Tin Factory" where Minnie Steuer, my grandmother, worked in 1900, I wondered?

The now-defunct company claimed infamy with a piece of history's most distasteful advertising. The Raymond factory had the audacity to hawk their wares in a lithograph, a poster depicting President Lincoln's funeral leaving New York City Hall. The ad depicted a banner in the sky floating over the procession bearing these words:

"W. M. Raymond Manufacturing Company, Proprietors and Manufacturers of Metallic Burial Cases and Caskets, 348 Pearl Street."

A patch of woods separating Winfield from its neighboring community also bore a dark reputation. "Winfield's Woods" were also referred to as "Suicide's Paradise," since legend told that the woods were a popular spot for despondent early colonists to end it all.

Even *Victorious America*, the War Memorial Sculpture by James Novelli, had a rough time in Winfield. The sculpture was placed in the town plaza in 1926 as a tribute to those who had lost their lives in WWI. The statue lost her place in 1939 when a new highway cut through the center of town. After being moved to a nearby location, the monument was covered in graffiti, had her head cut off, and was hit by a car three times.

Victorious America finally gave up. She remains in storage awaiting restoration funds; but even if that never happens, she, much like my mother, would no longer have a place to call home. Winfield has been buried under steel rails, paved over by highways. Whatever remained was absorbed by the neighboring communities of Woodside and Maspeth.

Research, usually revealing hard, reassuring facts, had further unsettled me. I realized that my mother began her life in a town where everything familiar was rapidly becoming strange and where once, everyone knew all the neighbors, but not anymore—a place where death was a specialty, a significant part of the town's persona, and the mainstay of their future. Ironically, although Winfield was an active industrial center in the early 1900s, by the end of the Second World War, it disappeared from the map entirely.

I sat in front of my computer screen in a daze. My mother's hometown was gone; and even while it existed, Winfield had been a place haunted by death. Could this be why she had preferred not to talk about it?

No, there had to be something more to my mother's reluctance to reminisce. Perhaps it had nothing to do with the town itself. But it seemed Winfield might have been a perfect place for a secret to be born. Maybe the town did a disappearing act out of respect for my mother's family, aiding them in their efforts to obliterate a story they'd rather not have told. I wondered if that mystery held the answer as to how my mother came into this world.

How could I possibly feel whole if my mother either didn't know her own family history, or was hiding some dark secret about it? The lack of details, the subtle smudging over of my maternal history, was responsible for my feeling of being incomplete. Now that I'd faced the elephant in the room, the truth suddenly became painfully clear.

I felt like half a tree because that's all I had in regard to family. Half a tree.

Floozy

July 1998. In almost consecutive breaths, my daughter graduated high school and announced she was moving out. Her best friend, Carla, had already secured a new apartment only a few miles from the University of South Florida, where Susie was to begin classes in the fall. The campus was relatively close to our home—less than an hour away. We'd hoped she would commute. But Susie had earned a full scholarship and thus her independence. She'd wasted no time finding a part-time job near the college. The news of her move was hard to take, but a threshold we knew, as parents of maturing children, we'd have to cross sooner or later.

She'd planned her move while my husband and I were on vacation, five states away. Susie reasoned it would be easier on everybody that way. There would be no tearful witnesses—her father, me, or her younger twin brothers—as she boxed up everything she owned and carried it out the front door. We left for our annual ten-day cross-country trek, knowing that home would be very different when we returned.

I caught her very few times on the phone during the week we were gone. When I did, she sounded as though she was either too busy to talk or had a mouth full of Burger King's finest. We rationalized: moving is a hectic business, and exciting too, especially this first "big" move out of Mom and Dad's house.

The day we got home, I couldn't reach Susie on her cell phone. I called Carla's apartment. That's when reality popped up, like an ugly clown out of a box.

"Hello? Hi, um, is Susie there? I guess I must have the wrong number."

"No, she's here," a deep male voice answered. After some whispers, no doubt muffled by a hand over the receiver, my daughter came on the line.

"Hi, Mom. You guyth home already?"

"Yeah, we got home last night. Who answered the phone? And why are you lisping?"

"Oh, that was Sammy. He's Carla's boyfriend." Susie cleared her throat. She sounded weird. "I just woke up from a nap. I'm fine, Mom. Really."

She drove home to see us that night, clearly skittish but decidedly defiant. She had two surprises for us. The first was that in our absence, she'd declared independent ownership of her body. She flaunted a tattoo at the base of her spine, and her brand-new piercing—of her tongue. That explained the lack of telephone conversation while we were in Texas. After a tongue piercing, apparently the victim is more

114

or less speechless for a few days while her tongue swells to fill her oral cavity.

Silly me. I was worried her slurred speech meant she'd been drinking.

But that surprise wasn't the big one. Susie announced proudly, now that all of her belongings were safely relocated, and she had permanently broken the umbilicus, it was not Carla she'd moved in with. It was Carla's boyfriend Sam—ex-boyfriend, to be exact. We were shocked. All through high school, Susie enjoyed a large circle of friends, male and female. She had never once mentioned a boyfriend.

While I stood with my jaw slack, my husband exploded. He ranted like a madman. He said things to her I never thought I'd hear him say to anyone, let alone his only daughter. Of course, Susie had already moved out, but he ordered her out of his house again, NOW. He didn't want "some cheap piece of trash" under his roof. He screamed hideous condemnations from the front porch, as she sobbed, leaning on the front bumper of her car, clutching the keys to her chest. Her father declared, in no uncertain terms, that he never wanted to see her again.

Shouting back through tears, Susie kept repeating, "But Daddy, I didn't do this to hurt you." Then, turning to me, "Mommy, I love you."

Her tires squealed out of the driveway. As the echo subsided, my husband broke down. He acted as though Susie had died.

"I've lost my daughter. She's as good as dead. I don't ever want to see her again."

I held my own pain inside my chest, like an invisible shotgun wound. I knew I had to be the strong one for both of us. Betrayal is never easy to accept, especially since I'd always felt so close to Susie. I'd had a more realistic view of the young woman she was becoming. Naiveté or denial, my husband still thought of her as his little girl.

Susie clearly had a mind of her own, and an emerging undeniably wild streak. Nobody could tell her what to do, although many times she feigned submission for her father's benefit. But I'd thought Susie and I shared every secret. I was mistaken. Right there in our family home, while I was frying chicken and folding laundry, she had been developing into a woman, one who'd now claimed a brassy independence and her very own sexuality. Although I shared my husband's pain, I felt my wound went deeper.

I had no one to turn to. I had no sisters. Since I'd married twenty years earlier, my girlhood friendships had fallen away. I'd become so involved with my family, balancing home and career, soccer games and spelling bees, I didn't take time for a social life of my own. I hadn't needed a confidante. I had my husband; and as she'd matured, I'd had my daughter. Now Susie was gone. And I could clearly see that in this situation, my husband couldn't help me—or me him.

I needed a female shoulder to cry on. I needed my mother.

But my mother was dead. I had no sisters, and Aunt Charlotte had been dead since I was seventeen. On that very black day in August of Susie's eighteenth year, the very same year we laid my mother in the ground, I felt more alone than in my entire life.

"I'm going for a ride." I finished the dinner dishes, then snatched the car keys off the hook near the kitchen door and didn't hesitate when my husband croaked,

"Going where? I hope you're not going to see that trollop. I've told you I don't want our family to have anything to do with her. We've got the boys to worry about."

I didn't answer him, just turned the key in the ignition, and threw the car into reverse. This was highly unlike me. It was obvious not only by the look on my husband's face, but by the shocked expressions from my twelve-year old twin sons who abandoned shooting hoops in the back yard to watch my car slide away into the street.

If it is possible to experience a sense of relief while in a graveyard, that's what I felt that night. I needed to see my mother, and I knew exactly where she was.

Veterans' cemeteries are such peaceful places. I guess that's a stupid statement; of course, cemeteries are peaceful—everybody there is dead. The veterans' cemetery where my parents are buried is in rural north Florida. When you turn into the landscaped entrance, it's comforting how they are so well tended. The flower beds are brilliant no matter what the season. The lawns between the numbered sections are as meticulously groomed as a golf course. It was evening but still late summer; so although the sun was dipping low behind the tall trees, there was still plenty of soft light to help me locate the right stone.

In veterans' cemeteries all the stones are identical, so unless you read the names carved into their surface, you can't be sure you're at the right place. The soldiers' names are on the front of the stone; their spouses' on the back. My mother's name, even though she'd passed before my dad, was carved behind. I dropped to my knees and grasped the gray- veined marble with both hands. It was still warm from its day in the sun. Sliding down, I rested my head on the curved upper edge. That's when I let the tears come.

I didn't speak aloud. I didn't need to, since I knew my mother could hear what was in my heart. She knew why I was there. I don't know how long I sat on her grave, my tears streaming over the warm stone. In life, as I'd grown older, my mom and I had grown further and further apart. But there are some subjects only a mother and daughter understand. When I made my way back to the car in the twilight, the crickets sang around me, and I had my answer.

***

Clark and I had spent the morning cruising the shopping malls in Tampa.

"I saw an ad about Burger King's new fish sandwich. I'd like to stop on the way home and try one, Hon. You hungry?"

My husband raised an eyebrow, since I usually scowled when the kids insisted on fast food. "Sure," he said. "Is there a Burger King on

Dale Mabry?"

Of course, I knew there was. It was right around the corner from the apartment complex, where Susie and her new roommate had been living now for almost two months, the longest two months of my life. I'd kept in touch with her by phone, secretly. My husband only occasionally mentioned his estranged daughter, and those conversations ended badly. Whenever her name came up, he'd spew a few foul comments, shake his head sadly, and fall silent. His foul mood lasted for the rest of the day.

I'd told Susie to meet me at Burger King at 2:00. I was so afraid my husband would notice her grape- purple Sunbird in the parking lot. But it was Saturday afternoon, and the lot was full. Even I didn't see her car. I was afraid she'd chickened out, changed her mind.

But Susie was there, tucked alone in a corner booth at the far end of the restaurant with her hands bound in a tight ball atop the orange table. I saw her first. I took my husband's arm and guided him in that direction. But when he saw her, he stopped and whirled.

"I can't believe you're trying to do this. I've told you—she's dead to me. I don't want anything to do with her."

I knew Susie couldn't hear his hissing words, but I could see her face crumple from clear across the room. I tightened my grip on his arm. Then I did something I'd seldom done in almost twenty years of marriage.

Up until that day, I'd been okay with playing the same role as my mother did in her marriage—obedient, compliant, non-confrontational. But now, we were talking about my baby girl. It was time I took a stand.

"Look, you need to realize something. This is not only your daughter—she's my daughter too. She's a part of me, a very important part, and one I'm not willing to give up."

First shock, then fury colored his face. A ball of anguish rose in my throat, but I swallowed and continued, "You need to accept your

118

daughter as a grown woman. She has the right to live as she pleases."

He shook his head. "Not under my roof. Not by my rules. I didn't raise a tramp. She's a floozy."

That did it. My anger flared, and I grabbed both of his arms and gave them a shake. "She's not a tramp or trollop or a floozy. And she's not under your roof any longer. She's your only daughter. You might be willing to lose her, but I am not." I stormed away toward my daughter who sobbed into her hands.

He walked out. Susie and I watched his truck screech out into midday traffic. I held her, and we cried. After a little while, I went up to the counter and ordered us both a coffee. I put extra sugar and cream in hers and carried them back to our table.

"Why is he like that?" she squeaked.

"He's old school, Susie. You've always known that. He'll come around." I said the words, but I wasn't sure I believed them. My husband was almost a generation older than me. He was old-fashioned, a lot like my father. If I'd done what Susie had, I don't think my father would ever have forgiven me. In fact, my dad probably would have reacted the very same way.

Daddy would never tolerate a floozy.

About thirty minutes passed. We didn't see the truck pull back into the parking lot, but we both looked up when the door swung open, and Susie's father walked in. He froze alongside the life-sized cardboard cutout of the Burger King. I could see he had been crying. After an agonizing moment, I nudged Susie.

"Go give your Daddy a hug."

***

My husband and I attended a baby shower this past summer. The invitations were adorable, covered with blue polka-dots and baby monkeys, and announced the impending arrival of a baby boy. Isn't modern technology wonderful? The grandparents were very good friends of ours and lived around the corner. Breaking tradition, they invited not just ladies but couples, and held a lovely barbeque in their backyard.

The shower was non-traditional in more ways than one. The invitations clearly listed the parents as having two distinctly different last names. No hyphens, no explanations. I was curious, so I mentioned it to another of our close friends when we arrived.

"I see they have maintained their own last names." "Yes," she replied. "They've decided not to marry."

The back yard was decorated to the nines, with blue balloons and streamers everywhere; the theme of "monkey" carried through ad nauseam. The mother-to- be looked about to burst. The gift table overflowed with I'm sure at least one of everything on her gift registry, plus a basket full of envelopes. It was one of the most beautiful, lavishly supported baby showers I've ever attended.

This baby would be born with huge welcome, pride, and fanfare. And to parents who were not legally married.

Oh, how a hundred years or so changes things. Back in 1921, when my maternal grandmother discovered she was pregnant—out of wedlock—instead of joy and anticipation, she was wracked with horror and shame. I imagine months of desperation, a grasping for excuses, and a quest for some way to make the baby acceptable to society. That baby was my mother. Throughout her life, she carried her own invisible tattoo—she was branded "illegitimate."

By today's standards, what my mother endured seems a form of child abuse.

The world I raised my daughter in was more than decades different from Grandma's. Susie's generation of women were free. She embraced her independence; she made that perfectly clear the day she hit us with a tattoo, a tongue piercing, and a male roommate—all in one shocking dose.

The first hurdle was the most painful, not only for Daddy, but for all of us. But once Susie severed the cord, we gradually began to accept, and respect, our daughter as a woman. Her own woman. She was no longer just our little girl.

And where did that leave me, as her mother? I had to decide: either let her go and keep her close, or clutch frantically and drive her away. Although we were raised in different times with different rules, I decided to accept, and respect, my daughter as her own person. It was no longer my job, nor my privilege, to condone or defy her way of life.

I decided to give up my little girl and embrace the woman who would become my best friend.

Carmen

"So, tell me again why I have to wear black? This isn't a funeral, Susie. It's a happy occasion. You're graduating college, for God sakes. This is a celebration!"

My daughter rolled her eyes in that same melodramatic way she'd been doing since she was nine. "Mom . . . think black and slinky—that's what all the businesswomen in Tampa wear for cocktails. And this party is in a *cocktail lounge*." She cocked one hip and rested a fist there. "At a very upscale restaurant."

"But it's a graduation party, not a cocktail hour."

"I know, Mom. But the people I've invited are all patrons of Ivey's bar—they're not kids. They're my regulars."

Ivey's was one of the more exclusive Italian restaurants in Tampa and where Susie had spent every midnight hour for the last six years. All the regulars knew her by name. She was the youngest girl Ivey's had ever had running their lounge. In just a few years, she had worked her way up from hostess to head bartender.

She'd made it. As tenacious as her dad, as persistent as her mom, our little Susie stuck it out and achieved her college degree.

Of course, we held her graduation party at Ivey's, in the upstairs private room. Ironically, the guest list included very few of her classmates. Susie wanted to celebrate with the people she considered friends; the bankers, attorneys, stock brokers, accountants, and real estate agents of Tampa Bay. They all made Ivey's a regular stop on their way home.

"Besides, Mom, don't you think the gifts I'm gonna get will be a lot better coming from my regulars? These people have arrived, man, and they rock. They've all got bucks, and they all love their little Susie."

The Ross clothing store on Dale Mabry wasn't fancy, made more obvious by the presence of shopping carts. But they have a huge and modestly priced selection. We screeched up to the dressing room, the cart's one errant wheel protesting loudly. The already large eyes of the thin, black girl manning the dressing room grew even wider.

"We only allow eight garments at a time," she warned with a distinctive Southern twang.

Susie didn't even look up from the cart as she gathered an armful. "Yeah, well there are two of us." Her tone was flat, almost scolding. "That makes sixteen, Hon. I don't think we have quite that many."

Susie carried one stack of outfits, I the other, and we made our way back to the largest cubicle in the dressing area, the one with the blue and white wheelchair sign on the door. Squeezing through the opening with her armload of goods, Susie commented, "You're old, Mom. We can use this one."

"Thanks, bitch."

The next hour was invigorating. Repeatedly putting clothes on and taking them off was exercise. I felt like a stripper stuck on rewind because every outfit Susie had picked out for me looked like one a stripper would wear.

Well, maybe not a stripper, but a floozy for sure. (Thanks, Dad, for this descriptive moniker.) Every outfit I squashed into was too clingy, too tight, too low cut, or too short. Every time Susie zipped up the back or I buttoned up the front, she stepped back, one hand on her hip, and squinted her huge eyes. She swooned, "Ooh, now that's pretty cute."

"Susie, I'm not twenty-something anymore."

"No shit. That's why we're in the handicapped cubicle."

"No, seriously, Suse. I can't wear stuff like this. I look terrible. I look fat and old."

"No, you don't, Mom. I'm telling you. This is the stuff all the women your age wear in the bar. They're not all skinny, and they're not floozies. They're sophisticated, educated, savvy businesswomen."

"But I don't feel comfortable."

Susie let out one of her drama queen sighs. "I need a cigarette."

We took a ten-minute smoke break outside on the sidewalk. She smoked, I watched.

"When are you gonna quit that, anyway?"

"Don't start, Mom. I've been under a lot of pressure lately." She turned to blow smoke over one shoulder.

"But it's all over now. You're graduating. You've got your degree."

"Yeah, and now it's time for me to look for a real job. No more playing pretty bar rag and making big bucks for flashing cleavage around."

I blinked but was used to my daughter's brass. "You don't sound too happy about that."

"No, I'm ready to move on. I've done a good job for Ivey's. But it's time to leave." She took a long drag on her cigarette, blowing the smoke out with the words, "Before they replace me."

"And why on earth would they replace you?" "Because I'm getting too old."

"What?"

"Yeah, Mom, the crowd that comes in—they're a lot of older, frumpy businessmen. They like scenery while they sip their Crown and Cokes. They want to look over the bar and see that 'almost looks too young to be legal' stuff leaning down to scoop ice into their glasses."

"I don't know if I want to hear about this." I couldn't help but wonder where this foreign creature came from. Her confidence was inspiring, but her brassiness didn't ring true to the way I'd raised her. Although I'd grown to be more outgoing and daring than my mother, Susie made both of us look like nuns.

"It doesn't matter," Susie said, bending to crush her cigarette out on the sidewalk. "I'm done with school; I've got my degree. It's time to look for a real job. But first, we've got to find you something to wear to this party."

"And what variation on the black theme are you wearing, anyway?

"I'm the guest of honor, Mom. I can wear anything I want to. I'm supposed to stand out."

Another hour, another cart full of outfits—all black—and another exhausting session in the dressing room. I still hadn't found anything I could wear in front of strangers.

Or, God forbid, my *mother-in-law*.

"Have you forgotten that Nana is going to be there?" "Oh, Mom, Nana won't even notice what you have on.

She'll be too busy schmoozing with all the handsome suits."

Now it was my turn for the theatrical sigh. "I just don't know. I can't wear this kind of stuff. I feel cheap. I feel ridiculous."

"Well, you don't look ridiculous. You look . . . appropriate. You'll fit in with the rest of the crowd just fine."

"Can't we just take one more look around?" Another monumental sigh.

The last trip through the racks, I did the choosing.

"What about this? This is snazzy. It's colorful, and it looks . . . well, it looks more age appropriate."

"It looks like something you'd wear to church, Mom." Susie rolled her eyes. "Not even church . . . a church picnic."

The store was closing in fifteen minutes. The girl at the dressing room gave us that, "I just want to get out of here on time" look, but I knew this would be our final trip. Now, the outfit draped over my arm said me.

"Look, Mom, I'm not going to argue with you. I understand. If that's what you feel comfortable in, then that's the right choice. God knows, I wouldn't want you to feel out of place."

A few days later, all the decorations were hung, the multicolored centerpieces set. I got there early to put the finishing touches on the upstairs room at Ivey's. I was relieved to see our personal bartender for the evening had shown up early as well. She handed me a frosted glass of Pinot Grigio atop a tiny, square napkin printed with rainbow confetti. She was almost my age, and I noticed her outfit right away: short skirt, shimmery camisole.

All black. Of course.

I flipped open my cell phone and punched in Susie's number. She and her father had dropped me off over an hour ago, their mission to retrieve Susie's seventy-nine-year-old grandmother from Largo, across Tampa Bay.

"Where are you guys?"

"The traffic sucks, Mom. We've got Nana, and we're on our way back. We should be there in about a half hour."

"Well, hurry. People are starting to show up, and I don't know anybody."

By the time Susie and her dad slogged up the stairs, half carrying Nana, the room was packed, and the drinks were flowing. Nana was very appropriately dressed, wearing a pastel screen-printed tunic over spring green polyester slacks. You could tell she considered this a special occasion: there was glitter glued over the pink roses on the tunic. A little waitress who didn't look old enough to shave her legs was floating through the crowd in her classic, little black dress carrying trays of fancy hors d' oeuvres. I was pouring my second glass of wine into an empty stomach and feeling more than a little giddy.

"Oh, Fran, there you are!" No matter how long I'd been married to her son, my mother-in-law always acted surprised to see me. "Ooh, that's quite the dress, now! Don't you look . . . festive." She smirked as she shouted the comment, as if I was either hard of hearing or terminally stupid.

Susie stifled a giggle. "Come on, Nana, your seat's right over here, at my table."

The party was great fun. By the end of the evening, everyone kicked off their black stilettos to dance. All of Susie's bar regulars humored Nana, each stopping by in turn to make frivolous small talk with her sometime during the night. They humored me, too. After my third glass of wine, they even convinced me to shed my sensible leather kitten pumps to jump around on the dance floor. Susie and I shook it up to Journey's *Don't Stop Believin'.*

Photographs will forever memorialize the night. Susie, the guest of honor, looked elegant in ivory Capris and sparkly lavender top. The rest of the guests provided a homogenous backdrop, all flaunting their respective variations on the "little black dress" theme.

And then there was me.

My mother-in-law described best my carefully chosen dress. It was definitely colorful. Beneath a wide portrait collar, the full skirt sported hot pink birds of paradise in a bright green tropical garden. Nana waited for a lull in the music, when there were plenty of guests within earshot.

"You know, Fran, there was a movie star from back in the '40s that wore a dress like yours," she chirped. "What was her name? Oh, I remember now. Carmen Miranda! Yes, that was her. But you really need a hat—with bananas on it."

Ah, the hat. Now that's something my Aunt Charlotte might surely have added, had she been foolish enough to choose the dress I wore. But in my heart, I knew Charlotte would most definitely have not.

Charlotte would have been in black, slinky and slit to there, with ample cleavage in view. She would have teetered in stilettos, becoming increasingly unstable as the night wore on. Charlotte would have taken every smoke break outside with Susie and her guests. She would not have sipped white wine like me, but downed vodka shots alongside the men. Charlotte would have had no problem keeping up with Susie that night.

My mistake was trying to straddle the worlds. I was raised by a mother who persistently chose the side of caution. My mother was timid, the classic church mouse. I always thought she was that way because of my father. But looking back, I think there was more to Mom's ultra-conservative nature than my father's puritanical, almost dictatorial influence. It seems my mother strove, in everything she did, to be the exact opposite of the woman she supposedly adored—the woman she claimed was her beloved, older sister.

If the story as I was told is the true tale, they were only half-sisters. No doubt, genetics can be tricky; and even if they were full siblings, they certainly could have ended up completely opposite in spirit, in character. I can't help but question that. It seems to me now that my mother was always trying to undo something, make up for the way Charlotte was. It was almost as though she felt guilty. But for what?

Why did I insist on choosing a dress for Susie's big night that befitted a church picnic? Because it would have pleased my mother, even though she was already dead. Because, perhaps, I didn't have the confidence to risk dressing the way Susie would have liked me to, or how Charlotte would have since in the past, taking those risks didn't bode well for me. Or maybe it was because I didn't want to shame my daughter by seeming brash, cheap. I didn't want to look like a floozy. As it turned out, I risked embarrassing her for a completely opposite reason.

Was Susie embarrassed? Hell no. She was just like Charlotte.

Shades of White

Back when I made custom wedding gowns, my kids were still very young. Even when Susie was just a little girl, I'd always dreamed of making hers. But Susie and Eddie wanted to fly off to Vegas or the Bahamas and get married in their bare feet, with no guests, no fuss, no complications. Thank God, I was able to talk them out of it.

By then, part of our family—myself, my husband, and one son— had landed in Massachusetts. Susie and the other twin remained in Florida, but we didn't let miles split our family apart. We flew from Boston to Tampa at least twice a year to visit. When the wedding date was set, Susie scheduled an appointment at a bridal salon in Tampa for our next visit. We bypassed the many fancy, high-dollar ones, seeking instead a smaller, friendlier shop where Susie could try on some dresses to see what styles she liked.

Our intention was to shop for ideas—not a dress. Denise would be our personal shopping consultant at 1:00 p.m. As we pulled into the parking lot, we decided that Denise would earn a cushy tip if she was nice, since we didn't plan to be on her sales list for the day.

Susie was more nervous than I can ever remember. She dawdled long enough to smoke two cigarettes between her car and the front door, though we parked barely fifty feet from the entrance.

"Why are you so nervous? And when are you going to quit that?"

"Mom, stop! You know how I feel about all this frilly stuff. I should have been a boy. I may be a teacher, but I wear two dresses a year—one on the first day of school and one on the last. And I hate every minute of it."

"Don't remind me. Remember your Easter outfit when you were five? I spent umpteen hours at the sewing machine and went crazy looking for a matching hat. You were climbing out of both before we even got to church."

"I can't help it, Mom. Look. Here...this is me," she flicked her index finger back and forth between her denim short-shorts and faded Tampa Bay Bucks T-shirt, causing the ash to fall from her cigarette onto the sidewalk. "This is how I like to dress. I look cool. I'm comfortable."

"Yeah, but is that how you want to look on your wedding day?"

"You already know what I would have done." "Yeah, unfortunately, I do."

I realized then her wedding dress was not for her, but for me.

The bridal shop was a girlhood fantasy, blanketed in soft-hued carpeting. The mirrored walls surrounded racks and racks of clear-plastic sheathed froths of femininity. Denise sat down next to us on the padded bench. Two mannequins draped in elaborate gowns flanked the entrance.

"How do you want to feel on your wedding day, Susie?"

Denise was, as Susie later said, "the bomb," a term I could only assume, considering her enthusiasm, was a compliment. Denise's voice was soothing, and her questions were less like sales interrogations, but more like inquiries from a close friend with her psych degree. But Susie still looked panicked. She hesitated, eyes darting frantically about as if all the fluffiness would suffocate her.

"Uh...I don't know. Special?"

"Good answer! Every bride should feel special. But do you have a picture in your mind of what you want to look like on your wedding day?"

There was a long, awkward pause. "Uh, no. Not really."

Denise smiled at me, but neither of us said a word.

She probably had children near Susie's age.

"So, tell me, Susie, have you decided on color? White or ivory? Or . . . ?"

Susie's eyes instantly locked with mine. I had raised her Catholic, and tradition dictated a wedding gown that signified virginity. Whether it was a façade or not.

"Oh, white. It has to be white."

"Susie, look at those two dresses on either side of the door. The one on the left is white; the other is ivory. Now, I think with your coloring...do you have any olive skin in your background? Mom looks pretty fair, but—"

"Oh, that's ivory? It almost looks white . . . My grandfather was Italian, so I guess I might have some olive tones."

"Ivory is really white, too; it's just a natural white, like silk after it's aged some. Why don't we pick out a few in both tones and let you try them on?"

We had Denise's undivided attention for the better part of the next two hours, an afternoon that would have made Cinderella jealous. Denise pulled me aside as we approached the long rack of gowns.

"I'd like to see Susie's preferences at first glance without any influence," she murmured, a respectful version of "keep your mouth shut."

It was a struggle, but I remained silent. After picking out a half-dozen styles, Susie donned a strapless bustier and crinoline. Denise handed me a sleeve of wet-wipes if I thought I might "want to touch" and a box of tissues in case I might want to cry, and then pointed to a padded chair outside a mirrored and spotlighted showcase area. I listened to the tentative banter between Denise and Susie echoing from behind the dressing room door.

"You know, I'm really nervous," Susie kept saying. "I'm not

really a girly-girl. I wear maybe two dresses a year."

"The dresses you've chosen reflect that," Denise answered. "They're all very classic and simple."

Within minutes, the door swung open and there she was, sheathed from bust to toes in a swath of sumptuous white satin. I was too shocked to cry: in truth, too awed to say much of anything except, "Oh!" It had been over thirty years, but I'd been at this juncture before. The difference was that now I was the one watching with a box of tissues in my lap.

***

"Where will we go?" I asked my mom.

"They sell wedding gowns downtown at that fancy dress shop across from Tompkins. You know, the one upstairs."

"Will we be able to afford any of those?" "I don't know. We'll have to see."

I was eighteen, silly in love, and ecstatic to be planning my wedding. I'd been dreaming of this day since I was a little girl. Although I'd always loved shopping with Mom, today's trip promised to be uniquely special.

The bridal shop perched atop a creaky set of old oak stairs, on the second floor of a boutique that my mother and I had never visited. They sold things we couldn't afford, even if we did have a fancy enough occasion to wear it. I had overheard Mom lecturing my Dad before we left home that morning, in a tone I'd seldom heard her use before. This is my only daughter, and she's going to have a REAL wedding gown. I never did. This one is for both of us. We'll find a way to pay for it somehow.

The place smelled of cedar and mothballs, and the sun streamed in through a bay window flashing sparks off an elaborately beaded gown in the alcove. One minute I was wearing my blue jeans and faded T-shirt.

The next I was teetering atop a carpeted pedestal in front of more mirrored glass than I'd ever seen in my entire life. My mother sat behind me in a red velvet- covered chair with a box of tissues in her lap. I tried on only two gowns. The first one was brilliant white satin so shiny it made me squint. An elaborate, form-fitting design, it dipped low in the front and was encrusted with lace and pearls. A lot of skin on my chest was showing. It made me feel like a rich, old lady—a brassy one—on the opening night of the opera.

"Aunt Charlotte would love this one," I giggled.

My mother smiled and replied, "You're right. She would." Then she turned to the clerk. "Maybe something a little simpler."

I caught a glimpse of the price tag dangling from the armhole seam before the gown was whisked away. As the sales girl ducked behind the racks of gowns, I whispered, "That one was almost a thousand dollars, Mom!"

My mother blinked, her eyebrows rising slightly, but she didn't say anything at all.

The second gown was an older design, sporting an empire waistline, a style rapidly going out of vogue for bridal fashion of the times. Not that I knew the difference. There wasn't a bead or pearl in sight, no shiny satin or daring décolleté. Just yards of white organza and a bit of Venetian lace. The tag hanging from the sleeve said White, but age had tinted the color to almost ivory.

"This is a sample gown," the clerk said. "The design is discontinued, but it's a classic. I think it might be just about your size."

When she zipped up the back, it fit as though the little dress had been waiting for me. I stepped onto the pedestal and the girl I saw in the mirror wasn't me, but the bride I'd dreamed of. Layers of sheer fabric floated around me like a full-body halo. I wasn't sure if there was a haze on the glass or in my own eyes, as I struggled to decipher my mother's reaction in the mirror.

Her image was blurred, as in a dream, but I heard her words clearly: "That's the one."

***

Susie had disappeared inside the dressing room again with Denise in tow—literally—carrying the heavy folds of a taffeta train. Susie tried on many more gowns than I had. Every one she chose seemed similar, but there wasn't any one that seemed perfect. Perfect, I kept thinking. Susie can list all the details from all the different gowns, just like Alexis did. I can combine them into one dress and make her perfect gown with my own hands.

"This isn't like a fancy restaurant, where you can order a la carte," Denise's tone edged impatient as they exited the dressing room yet another time. I was afraid she somehow suspected our secret plan. "You can't choose one element from each gown and put them all together, unless you're going custom," she said. She paused, glancing from Susie to me and back again. "We don't do custom here."

Her tone had grown cold. Susie and I exchanged glances. Then, without another word, Denise disappeared again into the sea of racks.

"Listen," she said, appearing with yet another plastic-encased swath of ivory. "I want you to try this one. It's very different from the rest you've chosen. I know you said you don't like anything too feminine. I don't know why," she paused, smiling at me first, then Susie, "but I think you might like it."

The dress was a fantasy in ruffles. A ruched bodice bore

asymmetrical lines, and at least a dozen rows of tiered organza fluttered all the way to the floor. My first reaction was terror, as the design, as well as the slippery fabric, was a seamstress's nightmare. I knew well the horrors of dealing with organza, cloth with a mind of its own.

Susie's first reaction was tentative, though for different reasons. "I don't know, Denise. That's a little girly for my taste." I breathed a sigh of relief, but then cringed as she shrugged and added, "I'll try it. You certainly seem to know what you are doing."

Susie could see me in the mirror from the platform. The tissues were in my lap; but until now, I hadn't shed a tear. I'd been too busy studying the details on every gown, making mental notes of the design elements that Susie liked. I had a sketch pad in the car. Our plan was to draw details before we left the parking lot, since it would be unthinkable to do it in the store.

Until now, the entire dress selection process, at least to me, had been clinical, scientific. Strictly business.

It never occurred to me that Susie would find the perfect dress, already made and ready to go out the door. But when she emerged from that little room the last time, she'd transformed, just like I had over thirty years ago. As she teetered on the small, carpeted pedestal in front of more mirrored glass than she'd ever seen in her life, I blinked into her image on the glass. Her eyes locked with mine.

"This is the one, Mom."

Was it truly the dress she loved the most? Or was Susie reading my unspoken wish? Flickers of memory revealed the truth. At that moment, I knew I had chosen my wedding gown from my mother's eyes.

One significant moment; a small circle of my life, complete.

***

We sat at the bar called *The World of Beer* a few miles down the road. I sketched frantically on the pages of a pink leather-bound pad

I'd carried with us. I couldn't help but see the irony in all this. Mother and daughter, just coming from a bridal salon, sitting in a bar near two sweaty, slightly tipsy guys in Ralph Lauren Henley's who'd just slithered off the golf course. With Susie on one side, I could imagine Charlotte sitting on the other.

"Look, this is pretty close, right? There were six...no, I think there were eight tiers of ruffles down the front, if I remember right. And two of them were pleated."

"Mom, how much is it gonna cost you to make this gown? I mean, just for the fabric."

I calculated quickly in my head and quoted a conservative estimate.

"Mom, do you realize we can buy that gown for just a few dollars more than that?"

"Yes, I do. But I can duplicate this gown exactly. Wouldn't it be more special if you knew I'd stitched it myself?"

There was a long silence. Susie swilled a good third of her second mug of imported tangerine-flavored brew, her eyes dancing from Tiger Woods on the widescreen TV overhead to the pack of Marlboros she'd just slipped out of her tiny Coach bag.

"I don't want to hurt your feelings, Mom." She took a deep breath and blew it out through pursed lips. "I gotta go outside for a smoke. Come on."

We carried our mugs of beer out to the bar's covered patio. As I clinked the glass down onto the metal table, I blurted, "You don't think I can make that dress, do you?"

Her eyes flashed toward me. Sometimes looking into her eyes was like looking into a mirror: their color was the same translucent green as mine. "I know you can make me that exact gown—maybe even more beautiful and that it'll fit me like a glove. But you have so much going on in your life right now. And honestly? No. I don't want to hurt your feelings, Mom. It really doesn't make a difference to me whether you make it or we buy it. A dress is a dress."

"So, you wouldn't be disappointed if we just buy that one?"

"Are you sure you won't be disappointed?"

My smile of relief was her answer.

"Well, then," she said, reaching two fingers into her purse to retrieve her phone. "I guess I'll just call Denise and tell her we're on our way back to the shop."

Still Hiding

By 2011, we'd been living in Massachusetts over three years. I'd been back to visit the place where Aunt Charlotte lived, and the town where she was buried, only once since the move. But I was writing about her now—this new knowledge that Charlotte may have been my grandmother was driving me. I needed every thread of inspiration I could find to weave the scraps of memory back together. One somber, overcast weekend, Clark and I climbed into the truck and headed back to Bloomingburg, New York.

The town's name was deceiving, longer than most of its streets. The graveyard wasn't very big either.

We drove straight to the northwest corner of the tiny cemetery and stepped out onto the wet grass. A red pickup had followed us in, and the man studied us with knitted brows as he rounded the corner. His window was open, and a dark sleeve rested on the door frame, although steady drizzling rain had already turned my hair into spaghetti. When the truck's engine stopped, my husband took a few steps forward and asked, "Are you the caretaker here?"

"No," the man replied. "I just dig." He opened his door and got out. He was a large man, broad-shouldered with big, calloused hands. It was Sunday, but he wore work clothes, his pants and shirt the sturdy, sensible navy blue of Dickies.

"I left the backhoe out yesterday when I was through." He

141

motioned to the rust-patched, yellow machine parked on the side of the hill. "I was just stopping by to check on it." It was a lame excuse, and he eyed us suspiciously. We were strangers wandering through the tiny graveyard in the pouring rain.

We had scoured the cemetery for almost an hour. I couldn't find the flat, stone marker. It was as though it had simply disappeared.

"I can't find my aunt's grave," I told him. "What was the name?"

I noted the past tense of the verb—was. Also, not "her name," but the.

"Colwell. Charlotte Colwell. Do you think perhaps they moved her for some reason?"

"No," he shook his head adamantly. "Nobody here has been moved for the past ten years. But I know some of these names because, well, I see them when I dig. What kind of a stone is it?"

"There is no stone, just a flat marker. I was wondering if maybe it cracked from the frost, and they've taken it out."

"No. Nothing's been removed from here." He spoke with assured certainty.

The man wandered toward the backhoe but continued to glance over his shoulder. He watched us. What did he suspect? We were grave robbers?

Clark and I kept circling back to the same corner where we'd parked. I was so certain she was there. But as the minutes ticked on, the cawing of the crows and soft patter of the rain on the concrete slabs all around us made the quest seem increasingly hopeless. I'd been talking aloud to Charlotte for the past twenty minutes, scolding her for hiding from me, and pleading with her to lead me to the place where she'd been laid.

Now, I spoke to the gravedigger, who wandered back in our direction. "I was wondering if someone replaced the marker with a headstone, and that's why I'm not recognizing it." I continued to trudge between the graves, the hem of my pants soaked heavy and sloshing against my shoes. Every step had become a cold squish.

My husband had been so patient. "I've looked all through those down in the next section, Frannie, but I'm sure you're right. This is where we found her before." His adamant finger pointed to the patch of ground where we stood. We both couldn't be so wrong. But the longer we searched, the more I doubted both of our memories. The more upset I became, the gentler he spoke. I knew his leg was hurting by then, especially in the damp chill that seemed to emanate from the ground beneath us as much as from the sky above. But he limped on diligently, pausing every few feet to squint through his rain-speckled glasses at the ground where another worn marker patched the grass.

Now the other man was searching, too. His big, bumpy knuckles were crammed, though not quite fitting, into the front pockets of his pants.

"Maybe if we look a little farther down this way," the digger suggested, his voice soft, almost too soft for a man his size.

"No, she wasn't that far down. She was right up here, in this corner."

"We all get older, you know, and don't remember things quite as clear as we used to." His sideward glance wasn't mocking. His smile was kind, his humor easing the tension a bit. But I had begun to panic.

It didn't make sense to me. Three years ago, I'd stepped out into the May sunshine on an Easter Sunday morning and walked straight over to the marker carved with my aunt's name. That day marked almost thirty years since I'd been back to Bloomingburg. It was a tiny town whose name stretched longer than its boundaries: four corners and a traffic light, bordered on the north by the graveyard and on the south by the quaint Victorian house bearing the sign *Matilda's Snip N Clip.*

***

"Hon, I just want you to be aware: I'm taking Fran to get her hair cut today." My mother's tone was flat with a hint of belligerence unlike her. My father's mouth fell open.

"Oh no." He shook his head, staring at me. "Not your beautiful, long hair."

"I'm thirteen, Daddy. I've never been to a beauty parlor. I want my hair in a style." I raised both hands to my head, pushing my long brown waves up over my ears. "Please, Daddy. Don't say no."

Aunt Charlotte made the appointment in a tiny shop on the edge of the small burg, just a few miles from her cottage. Matilda was her hairdresser. My mother didn't have one. I could never remember Mom going to a beauty parlor. Her hair nearly reached her waist, but her golden brown waves were always neatly contained in a bun or braids. She never let them flow free.

The day of my appointment was gray and misty, such a somber setting for what promised to be one of the most exciting days of my life. As we wove our way down the twisting road in our station wagon, I leaned over from the back to chatter with Aunt Charlotte. The vinyl seat was cold and sticky under my fingers. My mother drove, hands clutching the wheel. She was a nervous driver. And she was unusually quiet. I felt Mom's tension. Charlotte didn't seem to have a care in the world.

"Sometime, Frannie, you and I will have to go shopping for hats," Charlotte said with a glint in her eyes. "Oh, how I miss my hats." She glanced toward my mother, and even in profile I could see the thought spark my aunt's face into a mischievous smile.

My aunt wasn't a pretty woman. She was so much older than my mother; it was hard to imagine her as young and attractive. My mother's features were soft. She had creamy skin and the most beautiful blue eyes. Aunt Charlotte had a funny crook to her nose, and she always kept her lips painted a shocking blood red. Still, even at her age, she was the diva. She kept her short auburn waves in a puffed bouffant and lacquered them fast with sticky mist from a tall can of Aqua Net. Her eyes were green.

She raised one hand to her hair. "When I worked in Greenwich Village, I had a whole closet full of hats," she bragged. "One to go with every outfit."

My mother kept her eyes on the shiny pavement, but I could see the corner of her mouth turn up. "Don't forget, Sis," she said, her eyes darting furtively toward my aunt, "how our mother loved hats, too."

I remembered the black-and-white portrait on the edge of Mom's bureau. "Oh, that's right, Mama. Grandma is wearing a hat in the big picture you have of her."

There was an unusually long pause before Aunt Charlotte said, "Hats were very fashionable back then. It's such a shame they're not so much in vogue these days."

"What's vogue mean, Aunt Charlotte?" I asked.

"It means stylish. Popular. When you wear something in vogue it makes people notice you. Even envy you a little."

"Will I be in vogue with my new hair style?"

She grinned and shifted around more in her seat. "Yes, Frannie, you certainly will."

"Her father isn't too happy about all this, you know." My mother's somber tone echoed the dreariness outside. Rain had begun to fall in earnest, the mist swollen into a steady stream of well-formed drops that bounced and splashed off the windshield. My aunt just folded her arms and thrust her nose up into the air.

"Her father will just have to get over it. Fran's a young lady now. It's time she started looking like one."

"That's just exactly what her daddy doesn't want, Sis." Mom's eyes darted back and forth between Aunt Charlotte and the road ahead. Her voice trembled.

"This is my birthday present to my niece. To celebrate her becoming a teenager," Charlotte boomed. "Her father will just have to get over it."

Looking back from over the forty years I've lived since then, I suddenly hear what wasn't being said in their exchange. A subtle reminder from my mother to my aunt: don't give away too many clues about our background, my childhood. At barely thirteen, I was oblivious. I blamed Mom's nerves on my trip to the hairdresser: the decision she and my aunt made, against my father's will. In his opinion, women weren't supposed to cut their hair. Or wear fancy clothes, makeup, or anything that might attract a man's attention, like a pretty hat.

I guess I know now why Daddy thought of Aunt Charlotte as a floozy.

The beauty shop was tiny, on the ground floor of an older two-story home. The side door was painted hot pink, contrasting sharply with the drab gray clapboard siding. A little bell jingled as we entered. Inside, the mirrors lining the small room glared, round bulbs rimming each one. The air smelled like the lotion my mother used to give herself a home permanent wave. A *Toni*, she called it. That was how Mom kept her bangs curled and up out of her eyes.

"Matilda, I want you to meet my niece, Frannie. I want you make her beautiful today. I mean, more beautiful than she is already." My aunt winked at me.

The hairdresser was younger than I'd imagined. Aunt Charlotte was already old—sixty at least—and I assumed that she had her hair styled by a woman her own age. But Matilda couldn't have been more than thirty. She seemed younger than even my mom.

"Do you have any idea what kind of style you want, Fran?"

I handed over the crumpled page I'd torn from a magazine. I'd been clutching it to my chest the whole ride to the beauty parlor. It was a picture of Farrah Fawcett.

"Oh, I think this style will look lovely on you." Matilda turned to my aunt. "She will need a curling iron, though, or maybe hot rollers to keep it fluffed. Does she have something like that?"

"I'll make sure she does."

I'd never had my hair washed by anybody else than my mother. I lay back in a chair that looked like my father's recliner. The warm water and Matilda's firm fingertips massaging my scalp were so relaxing. It felt so good I would have fallen asleep, except that I was too excited.

When Matilda perched me in a padded chair in front of the lighted wall of mirrors, I almost didn't recognize myself. My face in the huge mirror looked pale and small, sticking up out of a green plastic cape with big pink roses all over it. My hair was slicked tight and flat against my head, like a wet cabbage just sprouted from a plastic garden. I shivered as a cool drop of water slithered down the back of my neck.

But my trembling wasn't just from the trickle of water. The reality of what was about to happen was beginning to sink in. This change would be huge. My heart was pounding so fast, I heard whooshing in my ears. And the scrambled egg and bacon breakfast my mother had so lovingly prepared felt like a ball of lead in my belly.

My hair had never been cut, not more than the inch or so when Mom trimmed off the split ends. I'd never been to a beauty parlor. Matilda clipped sections of my wet hair on top of my head and used tiny, silver shears to snip off long strands. I watched every piece fall, seemingly in slow motion. I realized this was my hair— my long, beautiful hair—being hacked at, sheared off, and catching in clumps on the flowered cape.

I swallowed and blinked fast, trying to hold back tears. Would I look even uglier without my long hair? Would I look like a boy? What will Daddy say?

I searched in the mirror for Mom. She and Aunt Charlotte sat behind me, at the edge of the room in one of the pink padded chairs. Her brows were pinched together, her eyes following the fluttering of the scissors and comb, watching silently as my amputated locks formed an ever-growing pile at Matilda's feet. Was she sad? Or just worried? Her expression made my throat clench tighter. It was even hard to breathe.

Matilda said, "This isn't really a short style, Charlotte. I doubt her father will even know she's gotten it cut. It will just be fuller, fluffier."

"Oh, he knows she's getting it cut, all right. Daddy had both mother and daughter about ready to back out before they even got here."

"Well, you know how some men are, Charlotte.

With the long hair thing, I mean."

"I've never let that hold me back!" my aunt shrieked. Her voice echoed in the small space, bouncing off the mirrors and sounding much louder, I think, than she intended. My mother's face crinkled, and she dropped her gaze down toward the floor.

"You always have been the wild one, Sis," I heard Mom mumble.

"And what's wrong with that? I've never let any man tell me how I could wear my hair. Or anything else, for that matter."

My mother's smile was small, sad. "No, Sis," she said quietly, "you certainly have not."

***

I walked back and forth, up and down rows at the upper end of the graveyard so many times that the names started to sound familiar. Clayton, Bosnar, Brown. Miller, Raymond, and Decker. The wet, marble stones shone like new, even though the dates carved on their surface were twenty or thirty years in the past. On others, the engraving was so weathered, the words were hard to read. Many of the flat markers were partially overgrown with patches of crabgrass.

"It's not like her to hide on me like this." I spoke softly to my husband. I didn't want the man who dug the graves to hear. "Do you suppose maybe she's trying to tell me something? Like maybe she doesn't want me to write about her?"

"Oh, don't be silly," my husband replied. "From what you've told me, your aunt was far from a shy one." He paused to reach down and

148

lift a vine away from one of the headstones, so he could read it. "Still, it is odd. The last time we came here, you walked right up to her." He studied me. "You're shivering. You're gonna catch your death. It's time to quit for today. I'll go start the truck."

The man was closer to us now and heard. He smiled, and he fell in beside me, weaving through the graves. I wanted to check each stone just one more time.

"You walked right up to her last time, huh? Well, then, why don't you do it again?" His smile was warm and friendly, as if I'd known him much longer than just a few minutes.

"I wish I could." I smiled and reached out to touch the sleeve of his shirt. He was so nice, so caring to take the time to help us. "I really wish that I could."

The rain began to fall heavier, the mist graduating into droplets that made a pattering sound as they pelted against stone slabs all around us. I was soaked and shivering. My husband was right. It was time to give up.

"Is there a directory? One that might help us to find her?"

"Well, yeah, sort of. The lady who keeps the record book is pretty old. But you might be able to convince her to look the name up for you. I can give you her phone number."

"I'll get something to write on." I turned and headed back to where we'd parked. I didn't follow the neat rows of headstones this time, but cut across at an angle. I was almost to the truck, where my husband was waiting with the engine running. Not more than ten feet from the passenger door, a cross blocked my path. It was rustic, just two pieces of weathered wood tacked together with some rusty nails. White paint still flecked the rough surface in a few places where it hadn't peeled off. The handmade crucifix looked out of place amid the carved slabs of stone. At its base, nearly obscured by a mat of overgrown grass runners lay a flat stone marker. Only the last few letters of the name were visible.

I hadn't seen it before, even though I'd walked past it, and around it, maybe a dozen times. I didn't remember the cross the last time we'd come. Positioned as it was, between two adjacent graves, I couldn't even be sure who it was for. I dropped to my knees in the sodden grass and used both hands to tear away the stubborn tangle of weeds.

"Well, here she is." I couldn't keep my voice from cracking.

The gravedigger man was right behind me. I felt his hand, heavy on my shoulder.

"So," his voice was a solid, low rumble. "You've found who you were looking for."

"Yes," I whispered, "yes, I guess she's been right here all along."

The Book of Rings—April 2012

"Mom! What's that noise?"

My poor hearing was further dulled by wind. That sunny spring New England day, intermittent gusts were tossing everything about. The whirlwind of the wedding had begun. I'd picked up Susie from Logan airport the night before, just seventy-two hours before her big day.

Our schedule would have given an air traffic controller chest pain. Since Susie lived in Florida and the wedding was to be held in Massachusetts, most of the planning had been done long distance, via

Internet and phone—it had ultimately become my responsibility. After all, I was the one who'd talked them out of flying to Vegas.

We were days away and all the last-minute details had to be sewn up. We hit the road early Thursday morning, multiple lists in hand. We had an itinerary: florist, then baker, then on to the mall to pick up the attendants' gifts. Next was scheduled a visit to Periwinkle's, the site of the Brown-Stich wedding. We wanted to check on the details, such as ensuring the candle centerpieces sat on the proper color of linen napkin.

Susie seemed incredibly calm, at least more sedate than she was during our phone conversation two days earlier. But on this morning, I again sensed panic in her voice as she climbed out the passenger door of my husband's Tundra, though a hefty gust of wind swept her words away as she spoke.

"What's that noise, Mom? That hissing sound?"

She was shrieking, though that was not unusual. Susie shrieks a lot.

I met her near the front bumper.

"Uh, oh. I think we might have popped a radiator hose." Mine was a calm statement, more an observation than an expression of alarm. Yet there was that sinking feeling in my stomach.

"No, Mom, look at the truck. It's crooked. Oh my God, all the air is leaking out of the tire!"

There were worse places for a heavy-duty All Season Goodyear tire to completely deflate in less than a minute and a half. If it had happened five minutes earlier, we would have been hurtling along Highway 190 at seventy miles an hour. The tire would probably have exploded, and being a front tire, would have certainly compromised the controllability of the half-ton pickup, with me at the wheel. That could have been disastrous, since not only was I not accustomed to driving my husband's truck, but my own steel belts had started unraveling a few days earlier.

Susie said I zoned out as I stared at the fizzling tire. While she was waving her hands in the air and pointing to the rapidly increasing tilt of the truck, I said nothing. She said my eyes glazed over, and when she finally got me to say anything at all, it was, "I'll have to call your father."

"That's not going to do any good, Mom. Daddy's in Virginia or Pennsylvania or somewhere. What good is that going to do?"

It was true. We were fresh out of tire changing males. Clark was halfway back from Florida, driving our son Jesse and his girlfriend up for the wedding. Jesse won't fly. His twin brother Justin lived with us but was working in Boston over an hour away. Susie's betrothed Eddie was still in Florida and wouldn't fly in until late Friday night. I'd never changed a tire in my life, and although Susie undoubtedly would have tried, the tire's rim alone heftily outweighed her.

Thank goodness for AAA and Gerardo's. Being stranded in front of Gerardo's Bakery wasn't the worst-case scenario: free coffee and all the decadent Italian pastry you could eat. I sat at a café table, nursing a cup of black coffee and pushing around flaky chunks of apple pastry with a plastic fork. I watched Susie through the wall of glass. Dressed in her favorite uniform (jeans and a sweatshirt hoodie), she paced back and forth in front of the tilted Tundra with her cell phone stuck on one ear and her free hand waving in the air. Intermittently, she came in to check on me, joining me briefly while waiting for the mechanic to arrive.

"Are you sure you're all right, Mom? You look a little frazzled."

"No more than you were when I talked to you a few days ago."

"Well," she began, "I was ready to kill Eddie when I spoke to you that night. He's just been so casual about this whole thing. He thinks the entire wedding just miraculously materialized! Meanwhile, he hasn't lifted a finger. Even arranging for the tuxes was more responsibility than he wanted."

I frowned. "I was a little worried after we spoke. I had a

nightmare that Eddie didn't show up. We had all these guests, cake and food for over fifty people, a DJ and a Justice of the Peace and no groom," I said.

"Oh, I'm not worried," she answered with a cocky twist of her head. "I figure if that happens, we'll have one hell of a party anyway. Maybe the next guy I pick won't have so much special care clothing. We spend more on dry cleaning than on groceries."

A bright yellow-and-white tow truck pulled into the bakery parking lot, and Susie was up and out the door. In less than an hour, the crisis was over. The spare was fastened in place, and we were back on the road. Susie came to retrieve me, the keys dangling from her fingers. "I'll drive," she said when I reached for them. "The guy said it might handle a little funny with that spare on
there."

I remember thinking that I had logged a few more miles behind the wheel of that truck than Susie had. But my hands hadn't stopped shaking yet, though I couldn't tell whether it was from nerves or from the rocket ship ride to Sugar Mountain that Gerardo's pastry had provided. I buckled my seatbelt as Susie pulled out onto the highway, lecturing me. "You know, Mom, you don't do very well when Daddy isn't around."

"What do you mean? I take care of myself perfectly fine without your father."

"No, you don't. But it's not your fault," she quickly added. "It's because you never lived on your own like I did. You went from Grandpa's house to Daddy's house. You never learned how to handle situations like this by yourself."

Maybe she's right, I thought. I know I would have eventually figured out that the 800 number on my insurance card would have brought help for the flat tire. Sooner or later, I would have dialed it, recited the digits off my card, and the angel of roadside assistance would have rescued me. Although it was true that I had become dependent on my husband to take care of me in instances like these, I took great pride in accepting full responsibility for the tasks I did handle by myself, like the wedding. The planning, the coordinating of the details—I tackled the task with gusto, so Susie's day would be perfect. If it wasn't, it would be all my fault. I was very good at accepting blame whenever things went wrong. I was good at guilt. I think maybe I learned that from my mother.

I awoke early on The Wedding Day, a gloomy Saturday in April. The sky started out overcast and rapidly deteriorated from drizzle to downpour. Our home swelled with family, fuller than it had been in many years. All three of our children slept under the same roof once again, two with the addition of their significant others. There were dreamers in the guest bedroom, snoozers on the couch, and snorers on the futon mattress in the middle of the living room floor. And as they all began to stir that morning, most of them awoke with really bad headaches.

We'd all stayed up well past midnight pre- celebrating the upcoming celebration. The boys had polished off a case of beer, and Susie and I killed an entire bottle of Pinot Grigio. After a half bottle of Jim Beam, Eddie passed out on the couch. Although the first hour of the day was painful, by 9:00 a.m., we had scattered—Excedrin bottles in hand—in a half-dozen vehicles toward different destinations. There were tuxedos to pick up and salon appointments. The photographer was due at 4:30 at our house to take pictures of Susie's donning of the bridal gown.

Rain poured all day. When we got to Periwinkle's at noon to set up the place cards, we gathered in the lobby of the banquet room with water dripping off our hair onto the slate tiled floor. It was numbing cold. Susie and Eddie, along with the best man, Mike, and bridesmaid Tess, were Floridians, and the heat had yet to be turned on in Periwinkle's banquet room.

"It's freaking freezing in here!" Tess's lips were blue and her shoulders quaking. "Our gowns are strapless. Would it be poor taste for a bridesmaid to wear leggings under her dress?"

Susie giggled but had a worried look herself. "Well, mine's strapless, too. I sure hope they have some damn heat in here by tonight."

It was then that Eddie and Clark called to us from the other side of the room. They were standing next to the "sweetheart table," the cozy spot reserved for the bride and groom. Both guys were peering up at the ceiling overhead.

"Uh, there's a pretty bad leak over here. It's leaking all over this table," Clark said.

Eddie and Clark moved the table away from the steady dribble of icy water that was rapidly creating a lagoon near the glass wall of Periwinkle's Garden Room. Eddie had originally wanted a water view, but I doubted this was what he'd had in mind. Susie ran up to the front of the restaurant to get the manager, while Tess stood scowling with her arms folded across her chest.

"Why aren't there chair covers? It would look so much better if there were chair covers," she said, wrinkling her nose.

It was already almost one o'clock. The girls were due at *Nancy's House of Beauty* in a half hour.

"We can get you chair covers," Karen the manager said. "But no bows. We would have had to order the ribbon three weeks ago. How are we going to secure the covers to the chairs?"

Fifteen minutes later the Brown-Stich wedding party had again scattered. The girls headed for the hairdresser. The guys headed somewhere for food and therapeutic alcoholic beverages. Clark and I, father and mother of the bride, were headed for A.C. Moore, the craft store in downtown Worcester.

"God, I hope they have that much black ribbon in stock. We need over a hundred yards. We'll probably have to hit every craft store within a fifty-mile radius." I continued to wring my hands, as I had been doing ever since we pulled out of Periwinkle's parking lot.

Clark kept his eyes on road, straining to see between the slaps of windshield wipers that were losing their battle against the torrential downpour. The weather turned a twenty-minute drive into an agonizing thirty-five-minute crawl.

"We don't have that much time," he said.

I made a mental note of the fact that men only spew logic at the least opportune moment.

But the craft gods were with us. Within the hour we were headed back to Periwinkle's with every last roll of black ribbon A.C. Moore had in stock. Clark screeched up to the banquet center, and I dashed in through the icy sheets of rain. I thrust the bag of ribbon into Karen's hand and dashed back out. It was already after two o'clock.

My cell phone started singing the moment I climbed back into the truck.

"Mom, where are you? I want you to be here when Nanette does my hair."

The original plan was that my sister-in-law Terri, Matron of Honor, would join me and the girls at the salon to share the bottle of Asti Spumante I'd sent with them, chilled and in a velvet sack complete with plastic champagne flutes. Terri was already there. She'd arrived an hour earlier, armed with her camera to immortalize the event. The idea was romantic and sentimental. But on the other end of the phone, Susie sounded more practical than emotional.

"If you don't get here pretty soon, Mom, you'll have to stop and buy another bottle of champagne," she said. "Or you won't get any."

We made it to the salon, and we drank champagne. Aunt Terri delivered ribbon-wrapped boxes of beautiful bracelets she'd hand-fashioned for all the girls. We snapped photos and laughed and drank more champagne. We watched as Susie's long blonde hair was curled and teased and pinned. And when Nanette fastened the crystal tiara around the cluster of curls piled on top of Susie's head, something magical happened.

I looked down in the chair at my little girl, the one who'd always hated being a girl. No jeans, no T-shirt, not a ponytail in sight, Susie looked like a fairy princess. Back home an hour later, my house was filled with half-naked girls. I had barely had enough time to pull on my own dress, a beautiful magenta creation with a wide portrait collar. I was still combing mascara onto

my eyelashes when the doorbell rang.

"Oh girls, make sure you're decent up there. The photographer's here. His name is Joe."

Our house is a two-story cape with two bathrooms. The downstairs bath was occupied by a girl in strapless bra with eyeliner on only one eye. Terri was in my bedroom hopping around on one foot trying to slip on her spike-heeled sandal. Upstairs, there were two girls in the guest bath, one struggling with the closure at the top of the other one's dress. As Joe followed me up the stairs and down the hallway to Susie's room, I tried to remember that although he was tall, young, and cute, he was also a professional wedding photographer and was probably used to scenes like this.

I reached up to tap on the half-open door, but Susie pulled it wide, standing there in a strapless bustier and teeny little blue bikini panties.

"Come on in, Joe. I'm not shy if you're not," she quipped.

I grabbed the white satin robe off a chair and said, "Will you put this on please? Isn't that why we bought it?"

At that moment, I heard a wail from the bathroom down the hall.

"Mom! The hooky thing fell off my dress. The zipper won't stay up. Can you fix it?"

The voice was from one of the bridesmaids. Apparently, I was everyone's Mom that day. Lindsay was wearing a one-strap sheath dress that fit her—I mean fit her—so her own skin was jealous. The hook- and-eye closure at the top gave way from the shock. I used the emergency repair kit I'd packed in my purse before we even left the house.

Twice. Not more than ten minutes after I'd threaded the needle with black thread, I heard Tess wail from the bedroom where the bride was getting dressed.

"Uh-oh, the loops popped again. It's the same damn thing that happened at your first fitting, Susie. I thought the bitch was gonna fix these things."

Susie's gown laced up the back with an inch-wide satin ribbon woven through loops where a zipper would have been. The strapless design could be cinched as snugly as necessary. Susie's waist measured in the teens and she had no hips to hold the dress up where it belonged through a long night of marrying and merriment. When I popped my head in the doorway, Susie was standing with her arms wrapped around one of the posts of her canopy bed. Jess had the two ivory strands of satin in her hands, her face timorous.

"Mom, help!" Susie wailed.

It took only minutes to rethread the needle to match her gown. As I squinted through my readers to re-attach the silky loops, Terri murmured into my ear, "You said you'd wanted to sew her wedding dress. Now you can say that you did."

From that point on, my memories are jumbled and fuzzy. Time was rolling downhill, starting off slow but gaining speed until it ran out of control. When I try to recall the sequence of events, I get eyewinks, like bursts from the flash of a camera, like the stuttered frames of an old 8mm movie. One minute I'm snipping the thread on the back of the wedding gown; the next I'm kneeling on the bed next to Susie, fastening the comb of her veil to her crown. All the while Joe was flashing away like paparazzi.

Mine was the honor of doing the bride's eye makeup, a thrill I hadn't enjoyed since the day of her senior prom. I applied the shadow, then liner, and repeatedly stepped back saying "look at me" to be sure both sides matched.

"Look at me."

I was finished, but when she looked up at me that last time, I fell into a time warp tunnel. It was now, it was then. It was today, and she was a bride at thirty- one, she was seventeen and it was prom night. I blinked, and she was seven and it was the day of her First Holy Communion. In the next frame she was five, gazing up at me with limpid eyes that pleaded, "Do I have to wear this scratchy dress all day?"

I got dizzy then, and time caught in my throat.

But time wouldn't wait; it was time to go. Someone in the hall called, "The limo is here!" as I scooped the makeup tools into a pouch and spotted the Hertzberg Jewelers bag on the corner of the dresser.

"Don't forget these rings, Susie. Here, you need to put on your diamond."

I'd only seen Susie's ring twice, once in an online photo because she lived seven states away. Eddie had gone over the top on that purchase. It was a custom design of diamonds and platinum that would have made a queen jealous. But it was petite, and it was tasteful. It had to be, since Susie's ring finger was only a size four.

"No, the bride's mother is supposed to wear it to the wedding, until after the ceremony. That's the tradition." It was Terri who spoke, and the claim was soon seconded by other voices. I'd never heard of that custom. Still, who wouldn't turn down an opportunity to wear a ring that cost more than her car? I hadn't owned a diamond since Susie was about three, when the stone fell out of my engagement ring and was never replaced.

I do not wear a size four. The ring fit on my pinkie, but not well. It felt awkward since I never wore a ring on that finger. It kept catching in the stiff netting of the crinoline as I knelt to help Susie fasten her shoes.

I dashed downstairs with an armful of makeup bags, hair tools, a can of hairspray, and my trusty mending kit. But my Vera Bradley tote, the one Susie had surprised me with last Christmas, was not in its usual spot. I stopped in all the confusion to think just a minute. I remember, I thought, I took it with me on our last weekend trip. I found the tote in my office beside my desk, still holding my mini laptop, its power cord, and a brand-new writing journal. I scrambled to fish out these things and drop them onto my desk. My journal was in the bag upside down and flapped open, forcing me to grab at it twice. Frustrated and rushed, I dashed into the kitchen with the empty tote, but as I tucked all the supplies I'd left on the kitchen island into Vera, a stark realization hit me.

Susie's ring was no longer on my pinky finger.

Although a lightning bolt of panic struck, I took a deep breath and retraced my steps into my office. I searched the floor beside my desk where the bag had been, fighting all the while with the yards of floor-length taffeta comprising my dress. I shuffled the items I'd removed from the bag where they lay on my desk. No ring.

Terri met me in the hallway.

"Come on, Frannie, we've got to go. The limo driver is waiting."

"I lost Susie's ring."

Terri's eyes owled, but she quickly said, "Well, it's got to be in the house somewhere. You haven't gone anywhere."

Terri and I tore apart my desk, emptied the contents of Vera, and dumped every makeup bag onto the kitchen island. Lipsticks and mascara tubes clattered to the floor and rolled under the counter. I overturned my purse, rifling through keys and coins and receipts from the purchases of the last two days. The ball of horror in my chest began to grow, rising into my throat.

"Did you use the bathroom?" Terri's eyes were wider now, as my own sense of panic began to take hold of her, too.

"No. No, I came down the stairs, went into my office for the Vera bag, and came back out into the kitchen."

Susie was standing just inside our front door, clutching the furry stole around her shoulders with one hand, a cigarette in the other, which she considerately had stuck out through the half-open screen door.

"Momma, where's my ring?"

By now she had caught bits of the mumbled phrases passing between Terri and me as we proceeded to ransack the entire downstairs of our house.

"It slipped off her finger. It's got to be here somewhere," Terri answered. "It's here in the house somewhere."

The bridesmaids ran upstairs to search the bedroom where Susie had dressed. Terri grabbed my arm and pulled me into the hallway.

"Is it stuck anywhere on you? In your collar? In the folds of your dress here?" Terri was running her hands up and down my torso, frisking me like a policeman.

"Unzip it," I said, "I'll take the whole thing off. We can't leave here with it stuck somewhere in this dress, or it'll be gone forever."

I ignored my lacquered hairdo and meticulous makeup. I abandoned modesty, as Joe the photographer was pacing from room to room helping scan the floor for the ring. The dress went up and over my head, and Terri frisked my half-naked body, while I scrunched and creased every inch of the carefully pressed gown in my fists, feeling for a circle of stones. But there was nothing there.

"We have to go. She's late already. It's got to be in the house somewhere," Terri was trying to sound calm, trying to reassure me. "You'll find it when you get home."

I'd never been in a limousine with a bar. Tess filled the champagne glasses, and Terri thrust one into my hand.

"Drink," she said repeatedly. "You've got to calm down, Fran. You're going to ruin everything."

"It's okay, Mama. It's in the house somewhere." Susie shrugged and smiled at me. "Now just settle down and enjoy this, will you?" Susie was incredibly calm for a woman who was not only about to

162

commit her lifetime to one man in front of fifty-odd people, but who also had no idea where her precious engagement ring was. Snapshots of her in the limo holding a champagne glass in hand show her as cool and beautiful as I'd ever in my life seen her.

I, on the other hand, had literally melted down. Terri dabbed a tissue to my cheek where the mascara streamed. I struggled to control sobs, as I dug futilely through the Vera bag again and again, clutching and scratching my beautifully manicured fingertips into every one of the tiny compartments on the inside and outside of the quilted cloth bag.

The rain poured down as the limo made its way to Periwinkle's.

Heavy rain fell all night and succeeded in washing away most of the crises that preceded the event. The leak in the roof at Periwinkle's was fixed, and the heat was turned on. Beautifully draped and beribboned chairs ringed the tables set with lovely floating candle centerpieces. The lighting was perfect, especially at the spot where the vows were exchanged, under a white trellis near the towering Gerardo's cake.

I know very well that I am biased, but Susie was the most beautiful bride I'd ever seen. As I watched her walk down the aisle beside her teary-eyed father, I realized this young woman was the personification of everything I'd ever wanted to be. She wasn't like me, but she was a woman I admired.

The worry of the lost ring lay heavy in my gut, an ever-present ache even the champagne couldn't numb.

But there was nothing I could do. And so, I danced. It kept my mind from ruminating, eating itself alive with worry. I danced and danced and danced.

The day melted into the morning after. We got home from the wedding around midnight, and I stripped, showered, and spent the next several hours crawling around on the floor in search of the ring. Around three a.m. I gave up, crept into bed next to my husband who was snoring. He was still oblivious to the crisis. At six a.m., I was awake again, and as I slipped on my robe he rolled over and asked, "Are you going to tell me what's wrong?"

"I lost Susie's ring." "You what?"

For the next six hours the three of us—my son Justin, my husband, and me—tore apart the contents of our entire home. The ring had vanished. Of course, the more time elapsed between the moment it went missing and the present, the more I doubted my memory.

"Are you sure you didn't use the bathroom?" I lost count of how many times that question was asked.

"No. I mean, I don't think so."

"It was an accident. Susie knows you didn't mean to lose her ring."

Not meaning to lose a twelve-thousand-dollar ring doesn't ease the pain of having been the last one holding it.

My husband began to doubt my version of the events. "She's not sure what she did. They'd been drinking champagne all afternoon."

Champagne was only part of the problem. It was time's fault: the day accelerated crazily. My house became a fairy land full of taffeta and lace and crystals, punctuated by flashes from Joe's camera. Nothing had seemed real. The more I tried to replay the memories in my head, the fuzzier and less distinct they became.

Had I used the bathroom? Had I flushed Susie's beautiful platinum and diamond ring down the toilet? Or had the prongs of the setting gotten caught in the netting of the crinoline when I fastened her shoes? If it had, she had carried the precious circle with her out the door. The ring could have fallen out anywhere. My son was scouring the grass beside our front sidewalk in the brilliant noonday sun, when Susie and Eddie arrived in their rental car.

"You didn't find it yet?" Susie still seemed relatively calm. She was convinced there was a place no one had looked yet. But Eddie's eyes glowed with panic. As she ran up the stairs to her room, I turned to him.

"I'll replace the ring, Eddie. I know this whole thing stinks, but I'll pay for it. I promise."

His eyes remained cold. "That's not the point. It's irreplaceable, but not how you think." I could hear the desperation in his voice. "I had that ring custom-made for her. Created just for Susie. It's not about the money. What's pissin' me off right now is that your daughter is heartbroken. Yesterday she was a bride, and today she's looking down at her finger and her diamond's not there."

His words were a sword to my heart, yet in some strange way, a comfort as well. In typical future mother- in-law-from-hell fashion, I'd seen Eddie as selfish and materialistic. Sure, he coveted my daughter, but who wouldn't as a pretty ornament for his arm? His reaction proved me wrong. At that moment, I really believed Eddie wasn't concerned about the cost of the ring at all. He was hurting for my little girl.

The ring was not to be found. Several hypotheses were raised, from flushing down the toilet to catching in the crinoline. It was even suggested that someone had picked it up where it dropped and slipped it into a pocket, but this was quickly discounted. There had been no one at the house who couldn't be trusted. None of the guesses really mattered. All that mattered was that my daughter was getting ready to leave for her honeymoon, and her precious engagement ring was gone.

I had retreated to the other end of the house, curled up in the chair of my sewing room where I didn't have to face anyone. The bride and groom were getting ready to leave. No one was coming to say goodbye to Mom. I was hurt by Susie's avoidance of me. She told me later that she didn't want me to know how upset she really was. Even in her sadness, she was trying to protect me.

My son Jesse came in to try to comfort me.

"Mom, I know it stinks, but still, it's just a ring," he said. "It's not like anybody died. Come on. Let's go get some lunch."

"I can't eat. You guys go. What time is it, anyway?"

Jesse glanced down to where his watch ought to have been.

"You know what? Last night was a bad one for jewelry. My watchband broke, right there at the reception. I'll get it, and maybe you can help me fix it."

While Jesse disappeared down the hall, I returned to my office one more time. Dropping to my knees, I groped under the desk, running my hands over smooth Berber carpet that in reality couldn't have hidden a diamond chip let alone an entire two-carat ring. As I repeated the same process I'd repeated a hundred times over the last 18 hours, I heard Susie bidding a tearful goodbye to her father down the other end of the house.

Jesse appeared in the doorway with the broken watchband and laid it down on the cover of my journal.

"Do you think we can fix it?"

I was still on my knees, eye-level with the top of the desk. As I turned to look at the watch, a sparkle caught my eye, but it wasn't coming from the silver of his watchband. It was coming from between the covers of my journal.

I thought for the moment that I'd lost my mind. I was hallucinating from the incredible stress I'd been under for the last two days. I slowly rose to my feet and slid Jesse's watch off my journal. I lifted it and opened the cover. There was Susie's ring, lying on the first new, clean page. It sparkled where it was tucked, snugly against the black spiral binding.

My daughter's ring was hiding on a new, blank page of a brand-new writing journal. I couldn't have made this story up if I tried.

Wouldn't it be wonderful to possess a rheostat on time, a magical dial to adjust the speed of events? The good times, like summer vacations with the kids, special shopping trips with aunts or grandmothers or mothers or daughters, holiday gatherings, weddings—these we could slow down to linger in. Conversely the bad times, like those horrible hours after the ring disappeared could be fast-forwarded, or better yet, stopped and deleted. I would imbue that magical dial with one more power: one that allowed us to rewind, going back to do differently those little things we do without meaning to, the ones that threaten to spoil everything.

As I sit and click through the 409 digital photos Joe took of the wedding, I try to imagine what it might have been like to experience that once-in-a-lifetime event without the bolus of anguish in my gut. But the day wasn't about me. It was about Susie's day being perfect. I'm her mother, and it was my job to make sure that it was. I suppose if I hadn't lost the ring, I would have fretted about something else. In the end, all that matters is that her wedding was, for her, the day of her dreams. And so I am happy to relive my daughter's wedding vicariously, through the eyes of Joe's camera lens.

"I love you, Mom." Susie hugged me as she was leaving, minutes after plucking her ring from under the cover of my journal. "Please don't cry. It's all over now. Think of it this way—now you have another chapter for your memoir."

Scrapbooking

It's become quite the rage in recent years. At the local craft stores, what used to comprise a tiny area in the picture frame aisle now claims its own entire section. The age-old "family photo album" has graduated to an official art form.

It's a trend that will steal the fun from investigative spirits of future generations.

Why? Because the mystery will be gone. Today's family stories are chronicled, detailed as succinctly as in a history book. Memories are decorated with cutesy, little die-cut shapes that convey not only facts, but emotions. There seems to be a cardboard icon for everything imaginable, from baby booties to graduation caps. No longer will one's great-great granddaughter wonder whom the infant was, the one in the arms of the girl with the spiked orange hair and the half-moon tattoo on her shoulder. Great grandpa's name, Willy Dee, will be inscribed in neon-blue sparkle gel pen along the top of that picture, along with the date and time of his birth. A polka dot teddy bear and paisley print horsey will colorfully punctuate that vital information at beginning and end.

Nonetheless, scrapbooking is one of my goals for the future, when retirement fills my days with that big question "What do I want to do now?" I certainly have ample fodder for a scrapbook; but for the time being, in the words of my daughter, I'm a slacker. I admit I've been lazy. My years of memories, those evidenced on old, stiff Kodak paper, are layered undignified, ignored but not forgotten, in stacks of boxes in the upstairs closet— those years, at least, until we entered the digital age. Once pictures could be recorded electronically, subsequent snippets of my life were etched in some indecipherable sequence of letters and symbols inside the portable USB drive, that plastic-capped shard hanging from my keychain. Unfortunately, these are even more inaccessible than the ones in the boxes upstairs, especially to those who aren't computer savvy.

My husband falls into this category. He's a hard copy kind of guy. Thumbing through those boxes of photos is something he loves to do. Clark has been retired for a number of years.

"Oh, look at this one, Frannie. Remember the Cozy Coupe? Remember the time I hooked it to the back of the tractor and towed Susie all over the lawn?"

The Cozy Coupe was a Volkswagen replica, a gift from Grandma and Grandpa on Susie's second birthday. Bright red plastic with a yellow top, it was the original fuel-efficient vehicle: it ran on child foot power, Fred Flintstone style. When my husband flashed the picture before me, I smiled and glanced over the top of my readers, only slightly annoyed at the interruption of my dreaded monthly chore of balancing the checkbook. There they were, in full color, on a green sea of grass. Keep your feet up, so they don't drag on the ground, Honey. I don't want you to get hurt.

"I do remember how you drove too close to the edge of the lawn on the third trip around. Oh, was she mad at you when she ended up in the drainage ditch!"

Next, he fished out a large manila envelope.

"Oh, here's another good one. Remember when you and Susie took that dance class together?"

This photo was professionally done; and there we were, splendid in our glossy 8 x 10 glamour. Susie was about seven, all spindly legs and oversized teeth in her sequined red leotard. I am posed next to her in my matching getup, and all I can see is how my shiny polyester-wrapped thighs look gargantuan and that my thick, black eyeliner had started to run in the corner of one eye. Both Susie and I wore matching red plumes that stuck up from the sides of our heads, sort of like those elephants you see in circus parades.

Digging in the picture box is like stepping on a time machine set in reverse, especially since snapshots from my lifetime merged with the contents of my parents' picture box after they passed. Very old black and white images, now faded to sepia, on tiny 2 x 3 rectangles depict people I never met, some of whom I don't recognize. But many of them stood in front of antique automobiles that made my husband very excited.

"Who is this, Honey? This brunette standing in front of the 1943 Packard?"

He didn't really care who the brunette was, just who owned the car. I squinted at the image and thought hard. It was my father's sister, Madeleine, the one who died of anorexia nervosa. In this photo, she was far from thin, but curvy and seductive in her fur-trimmed coat, shapely legs emerging out from beneath the hem. She never looked like that in my lifetime. I remembered my mother showing me this picture and saying, "That's what Aunt Madeleine used to look like."

There are many pictures of my father's side of the family—my aunts and my uncle, some cousins and great aunts I hardly remember. There are pictures of Christmas at Grandma's house: that would be my father's mother. Every Easter outfit I ever wore is immortalized. Usually, I'm posed on Grandma's back porch next to my little brother, who looks miserable and bored in a miniature Mafia-style black suit, complete with bowtie. Mom went all out with my Easter outfits, completed every year with a slightly larger size of white patent leather Mary Janes, especially after I'd graduated out of the orthopedic shoes I wore until I was four or so. And there was always a bonnet. My favorite part of every Easter outfit was the hat.

There are few photos of my mother's side of the family in the picture box. My mother appears often after marrying Daddy, almost as though she didn't exist until then. The most obvious omission is Charlotte. There is not one photograph of the older half-sister who raised her, helped raised my brother and me, and whom we all adored.

The more recent strata of photos depict my recollected past. In many, I'm wearing a hat. Like Charlotte, I've always loved them. They make me feel prettier, somehow more special. A hat seems to draw attention to the one who wears it. Donning a hat, at least in my family, creates an incident. There are smiles, one of the guys chuckles, and then someone shouts, "Who's got a camera?"

There I am, with my best friend Loraine at her graduation party on a sunny June day in her father's immaculate back yard. Somebody captured us in a silly pose side-by-side. I was wearing my newest hat. It was pale pink with a huge sheer brim, the bands of netting and ribbon casting a concentrically striated shadow all over my face and shoulders. Standing next to Loraine, half a head taller than me, I looked like a character from Alice in Wonderland: the striped Cheshire cat peeking out from under a mushroom.

In many other of these old pictures, I appear astride a horse, a sport I've been obsessed with most of my life. Riding naturally required a hat, more for safety than fashion. While most kids were kicking around a soccer ball or trying out for the cheering squad, I was begging Daddy for riding lessons. I finally succeeded during the summer of my eighth year. By the age of fourteen, I was working at a local stable, exchanging hours of shoveling manure for minutes astride a horse. The ratio worked out to be about 30:1; but to me, it was the deal of a lifetime.

I came across a picture of a smiling blonde genie sitting on a petite bay horse. That would be me. I was about twenty-five and had decorated myself and my mare Cassie for the Native Costume Class of the big regional Arabian Breed Association show. I was Barbara Eden of *I Dream of Jeannie*. Decked out in red velvet and pink organza, I looked seductive in my pillbox hat and face-draping veil. Ms. Eden made the world blush in the 1960s by baring her midriff on national TV. I had to alter the costume's design for modesty's sake. I made the costume myself on my ancient Singer sewing machine. The motor looked like a huge, black bumblebee hanging off one side of the contraption and transformed the pedal-drive machine to electric power. The thing made such a clatter that my husband wouldn't let me sew when he was watching TV, even two rooms away.

Showing Cassie in another class, I'm all gussied up in what was referred to as a saddle-suit. This was a cross between a leisure suit and a tuxedo with way-too-tight bellbottoms. Again, I'd been forced to fashion my own when my husband whined, "Two hundred dollars for an outfit to show your horse in? We just can't afford that, Honey." It was navy with a matching bowtie that I wore with a baby blue shirt I'd found on a sale rack in Lloyd's. I spent hours at the dining room table after our then- infant daughter was asleep, cutting and taping a McCall's blazer pattern into the proper design.

Tradition decreed a saddle-suit be worn with a bowler hat. I went to Goodwill and found an old brown fedora. I took it home and steamed the hell out of it over a boiling pot on the stove. After getting the shape right, I got out my can of blue fabric paint. It took about a half dozen coats, but I finally got it to match.

My days of showing Arabians were after I was married and already a mother. Earlier in my horse-showing career, I rode hunt seat. As a teen, my passion was hurdling over brightly colored fences atop horses that were crazier than I was. My father shared my dream, that I would ride Grand Prix, qualify for the Olympics and travel all over the world. There are many pictures in the box of me dressed in traditional hunt attire: beige breeches, black Melton coat with matching velvet cap. In some of the older black-and-whites, I wasn't much older than Elizabeth Taylor in National Velvet. Until I was about eighteen, I paid for my riding lessons with the proceeds from my after-school job. I just didn't have enough for the lessons and the outfit for that big horse show, the one scheduled for a few weeks away at the barn where I rode.

***

"Daddy, this is my instructor, Henry."

Henry Barclay wasn't a handsome man, but when I was seventeen, he was my Adonis. He ran the riding stable in Chester, the next town over from where we lived. I had been taking lessons for about three months. I paid for them with what I earned selling 45s and LP record albums at Lloyd's in the music department, my after-school job. Daddy was paying for the roof over my head, my car, my auto insurance, and my gas. But the lessons, I was proud to say, I was paying for myself.

My love for horses, and my drive to be an equestrienne, was not something my parents understood. No one in my family ever rode a horse. We lived in a rural area, but there were no horses anywhere nearby. There seemed no logical explanation for my obsession.

"How serious are you about your daughter's riding career, Mr. Del Negro?" asked Henry.

My father was a salesman and was wearing his staid business face: the one that said, Okay, I've got this guy's attention, now what can I sell him? He thumbed his lower lip between his two bony

175

fingers, as he leaned over the lower half of the Dutch doors that enclosed Henry's indoor arena. I was sitting just inside, astride my lesson mount for the day, a gorgeous, dapple grey Thoroughbred that Henry called "April."

"Well, I'm serious about anything that has promise," my father finally responded. "Tell me, Harry, what do you think of my daughter's potential?" I cringed and hoped Henry hadn't noticed that Daddy misspoke his name.

Henry cleared his throat, but he did that a lot. He was a tall man, wiry and angular like my father, and smoked nearly as much. Henry had a booming voice that bellowed authority over great distances to wherever his students were, usually halfway across the arena on their way to the next fence. He had commented on my riding talent and noticed my appetite for competition since my first week of lessons.

"I wouldn't have asked you here today unless I thought your daughter had a lot of potential," Henry said. "She's quite an impressive rider. April is not an easy horse to ride. Not many of the kids can handle him."

I could almost see my father's silhouette expand. He stood up just a little taller and reached into the breast pocket of his shirt. Henry waited as Daddy withdrew a cigarette and lit it, the flame from his lighter causing April's head to lift and turn in his direction. Then Daddy spoke, his words creating a billow of smoke that made the horse's dark eyes blink.

"April, huh? If it's a boy horse, why do you call him April?"

Henry chuckled. "His registered name is April's Here. He was born on April 1st."

My father grinned and was quiet for a moment. "An April's fool, huh?" I could see him scanning the horse with his eyes, measuring him up as though he had enough knowledge of equine talent to make such an appraisal. Then he glanced up at me with that glint in his eyes that said, I'm so proud of you.

"Just how far do you think she could go?" he asked. "There's a competition class called Medal Maclay. It's for young riders under eighteen." Henry looked up at me. I sat staring at my hands, fingering the narrow leather reins. My knees were trembling against the flaps of the saddle, and I felt as though my entire future hung in the air between Daddy and Henry. "When did you say you'd be eighteen, Frannie?" Henry asked.

"Not until next year, in November."

"She's eligible to compete all of this year, and all of next. She could well earn her entire college education with the winnings from this competition, Frank."

I had a list, and I had an address. Kaufmann's Saddlery was located in Manhattan, a sixty-mile drive from where we lived; but for me, it could have been on another planet. I was born in the big city, but my parents moved out when I was a baby. I grew up in the country, in a place that didn't even qualify as a suburb. Everyone had their own plot of land. Air in the summer smelled like cut grass, not gasoline and diesel exhaust. I was accustomed to leafy shadows animated by the breeze. Angular, sharp-edged shadows had already dropped 29th Street into an early twilight, when my father turned our secondhand Cadillac onto the ramp of the parking garage a half block from our destination.

Kaufmann's was a horseman's dream world. The bell on the glass-paneled door echoed within as we entered, resounding off polished, wide-board flooring that gleamed as though it had been waxed just that day. The space was cavernous. An embossed tin ceiling soared to incredible heights that made every sound return a soft echo. A slightly musty smell mixed with scents of starched cloth and oiled leather.

Islands of garments floated on circular steel racks, some protected inside their own zippered plastic bags. Breeches with real suede knee patches were folded in neat stacks on tables. Boxes filled shelves rising so high against the walls, I wondered how anyone could ever retrieve them. A mannequin in one corner struck a proud pose in her plaid jacket with the velvet collar, a riding crop balanced between her bright red-tipped fingers. She wore a hunt cap in matching black velvet.

As soon as the door clicked shut, an older, balding man in a dark suit stepped out from behind the glass display case. I clutched the crumpled notebook sheet in my hand, the list I'd carefully inscribed in dull pencil that morning as Henry dictated.

"And what can I help you good folks with this afternoon?"

The man looked like a butler from an English estate and sounded like one, too. I shrank into myself, dropping my head and eyes and trying very hard to disappear. But I was the one looking for an outfit, and I would be in the spotlight. It would be me taking off my clothes at some point in this strange environment, albeit I hoped behind closed doors. I didn't see any females on the sales floor, only men who seemed much older than my dad. I kept my eyes glued to the shiny, wood floor beneath my dirty sneakers and didn't say a word.

My father cleared his throat. "My daughter here needs an outfit. She's going to be showing a very talented horse in some pretty big competitions. I need to get her red up." My father was nervous, too, although he tried to hide the quiver in his voice by notching up the volume.

"Well, we certainly can help you with that. What exactly will the young lady be needing?"

"Everything." My father declared. "Everything, from the boots up."

The next hour was frenzied and awkward. I didn't know what size I wore in real riding breeches or ratcatcher shirts or hunt boots. When I emerged from the dressing room the last time, my face was red, and I was out of breath. My thighs felt like sausages in the skin-tight breeches. A starched, high-collared shirt threatened to strangle me, and shoulder pads in my jacket could protect an NFL quarterback. The boots were the piece de resistance. I've always had rather short legs, and the stiff, black leather tops extended well above my knee joint. I couldn't bend my leg if my life depended on it.

"Oh, you really look the part now, Frannie." My father glowed with pride. The muscles of my calves screamed pain. I remember thinking, how does one wear this stuff and ride a horse? I tried to imagine mounting April. He was a very tall horse, and I a very short girl. I had to lift my foot high enough to slip into a stirrup that hung at just about eye level. The very thought of trying while wearing those boots made me wince.

The two salesmen were gawking at me in a way that made me feel uncomfortable. One of them said, "You folks aren't from the city, are you?" and then paused, his eyes so shiny it almost seemed as though he would cry. "Your daughter has such a pure, innocent air about her. You don't see that much around here anymore." I could swear I saw him lick his lips, at least once.

"No, she was raised in the country. A good, clean country girl," my father said, and I cringed. "Is this it? Is this all she needs to show Grand Prix?"

My father's naiveté must have amused the two Kaufmann's cronies, who I'm sure had helped dozens of daddies outfit their little girls for the big ride. But they didn't let on. They both just smiled as one said, "Well, she'll also be needing a cap."

The hunt cap. It's been a tradition for fox hunting parties for hundreds of years. Designed for safety and style, it's a minimal, scalp-hugging helmet with a short brim at the front to shield the rider's eyes from the early morning sun. It's constructed with a hard body, made of high-tech plastic nowadays, but is still covered in traditional black velvet as it has been forever. The gentleman at Kaufmann's climbed up on a rolling set of metal stairs to retrieve one in my size from an upper shelf lining the back wall.

His eye was accurate. The hunt cap slipped down over my scalp smoothly. He fiddled with the brim just a bit to be sure it was angled right, his eyes dancing over my face as he did.

"There," he declared. "Now she's fashionable, and safe as well."

I stood in front of the narrow mirror tacked up on the outside of the dressing room. I was trussed from head to toe in classic, customary English riding garb. Even to my own critical eye, I had to admit: I did look the part. My father stood behind me, murmuring proudly to the two men who continued to stare at me as if I were today's special on the lunch menu. Could I fulfill my father's dreams for me? Could I fulfill my own? One thing I knew for certain: I didn't have enough money to buy everything I was wearing. I turned to my father and interrupted his conversation.

"Daddy, can we afford all this?"

I will never forget the look of hurt in his eyes or the indignant tone in his reply.

"Well, of course, we can. Anything for my little girl." Then he paused, reaching down to check the orange price tag on the hat box. "You can pay for the hat," he declared.

I don't know how he paid for the rest of my outfit that day, but I felt like Cinderella. I never did get to show April at the big shows, nor compete for Medal Maclay. My chosen sport turned out to be a very costly one and required more expendable income than we had. But that outfit saw me through many years of small local shows and helped me earn a roomful of silk ribbons. Plus, the pride of my father, a prize that was always the most important to me.

I still own that hat. It has seen me through dozens of classes aboard many different horses. That velvet cap has witnessed moments of triumph and days of defeat. And every time I snug it down over my head, I remember that day with my father, the day he saw me with fresh eyes, not just as his little girl, but as an accomplished equestrienne. That day I believe, in some small way, he conceded that

Aunt Charlotte was right, at least about one thing: there is the right hat for every occasion.

For once, I'd found a hat my father approved of my wearing.

***

I stared at the black-and-white photo of the little girl, all dressed up astride a shiny horse. It's funny how photographs can transport you back in time. For a moment, I could almost smell the leather and oiled wood of old Kaufmann's, could almost feel my father's proud gaze.

Closer to the top of the box are pictures of my own family. My husband with hair, long sideburns, and wearing that green argyle pullover that I hated. There is one of me proudly side-posing, seven months pregnant with our daughter. After her birth, Susie's childhood is chronicled at almost weekly intervals, many images with my mother and father, whom she adored. Then when she's about six, she is joined by her twin brothers, scrunched faces floating in the sea of blue paisley that lined their matched baby carriers.

This box of photos chronicles my life, and the lives of my loved ones. But what does it say about me? Is there a common theme linking all the moments I thought were worth immortalizing in print? To be honest, the choice wasn't always my own, but maybe those are the snippets of my life that are the most revealing. The ones that caught me unaware, not posing, just being myself. I thumb through the pile, deciphering the obvious clues, and reach the most elementary conclusion: I'm a daughter and a wife and a mother. Now, let's elaborate.

I'm the daughter who grew up with a desperate drive to please her daddy. But by being more like her mother? No, I don't think so. Not me. I was more daring than that, and I admired, and envied, Aunt Charlotte way too much.

Was I the wife who has always tried to live up to that impossible, Mrs. Beaver Cleaver ideal, like my mother?

Was she that ideal wife? She certainly tried. Did I approve of the way she was so obviously ruled by my father? No. I don't think I did.

I'm the mother who did her best to raise a daughter and cantankerous twin boys, and then looked down one day and didn't recognize the young woman who used to be her little girl. She was nothing like me. Nothing like her grandmother. I realized my daughter was the reincarnation of a woman—a mindset, an unflappable (pardon the pun) spirit—almost a hundred years old. Like Charlotte, Susie possesses a completely independent way of thinking I never had the guts to openly embrace.

Who have I been trying to be all these fifty-odd years?

The pictures hold their secrets, revealing only latent images. There are no firm answers here, only birthday cakes and Christmas trees hovering over a sea of toys and crumpled paper. There are summer picnics and beach vacations, ever-flying kites on St. Augustine beach in July. There are prom gowns and caps and gowns. The snapshots hold no revelation as to who I really am, offering no real clues as to how I might fill out my half a tree. But there is evidence of love, and plenty of it.

And not all of the pictures recall happy times.

There is a small group of photos taken the year my mother died. In one snapshot, I stand with my arm around her then bone-thin form, just before her hair all fell out, and she got so weak she could no longer stand. A few photos deeper in the stack, she is no longer one of the group. It was taken on her front porch. The moment brands my memory, though I've tried hard to forget. We were all about to leave in the black car that would take us to her funeral. My father sits at center in his wheelchair, wearing his grief like a dismal shroud. My brothers and I, with our own families, are fanned out behind and beside him. The first family portrait after we lost Mom.

I have no recollection whose idea this portrait was and still doubt it was a good one. Surrounded by my husband and children, I looked even paler than usual in my black mourning dress. But take note: I was wearing a hat. It was my mother's hat, the only one I ever remember her owning.

It was Daddy's idea. He wheeled his chair to her closet door and pointed a trembling finger toward the box on the top shelf. He said Mommy would have wanted me to wear it. A small, black velvet pillbox with netting to cover the eyes, Mom had bought the hat to wear to her sister's funeral many years before.

My mother never wore a hat, not even to church. For that she pinned a white hanky to her hair. But for Charlotte, the day they put her in the ground, Mom had worn black velvet. It was only fitting that I return the gesture.

It's All in the Hat

I grew up less than a hundred miles from New York City, yet at fifty-two, my trip into Boston marked only the second time in my life I'd ever ridden the subway. As such, I was oblivious of the Subway Commandments. These are unwritten rules, akin I'm sure to Elevator Etiquette with this first commandment:

Thou shalt not acknowledge ye are crammed up against a bunch of strangers, like so many panties in a lingerie drawer.

Eye contact is not a good idea. Conversation is even more taboo. It only took me two days of riding the Boston subway to learn the ropes. But I am too much of a busybody to stare at my lap.

It was her hat that caught my eye, as I'm sure it did dozens of others that morning or whenever the lady chose to wear it. The rest of her outfit blended with the other occupants of that Red Line train during the rush hour commute. It was mid-January, a bad one in Massachusetts, with snow burying most everything, and temperatures hovering in the teens. Everyone wore the New England winter uniform: some variation of the Michelin-Man-style, puffy down jacket.

Hers was a nondescript color, a dark gray, and almost full length, reaching to the tops of her sensible, flat-heeled boots. She had a black canvas laptop case slung over one shoulder and carried a small brown paisley Vera Bradley in the other hand. Nothing made her stand out in a crowd. Except her hat.

It was a cloche, that helmet style so popular back in the Roaring

Twenties. The design completely obscured her hair, so I couldn't even determine if she had any. The front was pulled low, covering her eyebrows and reaching almost to the tops of her eyelids. The set of the brim caused her to carry her chin just a bit tipped up in order for her to see. She stood with more weight resting on one foot than the other. Her free, leather-gloved hand clutched the vertical steel bar. Her stance was almost haughty: an expression that snapped, "What?" with an impatient edge. Her lips were painted bright red, and her hat looked like mink, judging by the soft, milk chocolate color and silky sheen.

I've never been a fashion guru, though I wanted to be. I select my wardrobe according to three criteria: comfort, price, and does it make me look fat? Usually, but not necessarily, in that order. But I've always had a soft spot for fur. It's probably the result of seeing one too many Humphrey Bogart movies, watching Lauren Bacall slip sensually out of a long, white fox coat. I've always loved hats too, though I have, in maturity, lost the nerve to wear one just for fashion's sake.

This lady's hat was so out of place there, on the subway on a rush hour train on an ordinary weekday morning, I wanted to applaud her. The decadent accessory matched nothing about her outfit. If asked, she might have claimed she wore it for the warmth, although I'm sure it offered no more protection than the pink, knitted woolen cap on the girl standing to her left or the quilted down hood on my own sensible winter jacket. No, I'm quite certain the lady wore the hat to make a statement, and it most certainly did. A mute but unmistakable shout in the crowd.

She had the kind of look I'd always wanted. Chic, classy, confident. Yet somehow, I'd never felt able to achieve that goal, at least not with any level of certainty. Once in a while, on a whim I might have put together an outfit that "shouted in the crowd." But ever since I was about seventeen, the shout dwindled to a whimper. I chickened out, opting for more traditional, less flamboyant attire. I might dress up for the silent witness of my bedroom mirror, but I seldom made it out the door.

Guess I probably have creepy Harry to thank for that, huh?

***

I'm almost embarrassed to admit that the revelation—the realization of the possibility—that Charlotte could be my grandmother and not my aunt didn't hit me until I was fifty-two years old. And I didn't even come to it on my own. I was in a public place, sitting with acquaintances not quite yet graduated to friends. We had met in the commons of the dormitory at Lesley University in Cambridge, Massachusetts, where I was working on my MFA in creative writing.

There were only three of us in the nonfiction genre, class of 2012—Julie, Pamela, and me—and we were in the thick of our second residency. That evening, we were lounging in the abandoned common room of Wendell Hall on their comfortable sofas, sipping vodka tonics and discussing our final projects—our theses.

We decided to do a few readings of each other's work. I read to them an essay I'd written about finding my grandfather's grave, the culmination of my search for my mother's dad after she passed away.

"The most perplexing part to me," I said, topping off my second cocktail with extra ice from the bucket, "is that the man lived right around the corner from where my mother grew up. And another thing, my grandmother lied about her age on Mom's birth certificate. She put it down as thirty-nine when multiple census records show that she was in her mid-forties when my mother was born."

"And how old was your grandfather when your mom was born?" Pamela asked. She was the youngest of us three, fresh out of undergrad.

"He was twenty-nine. And I know that's true because I found his draft card from 1918. That's how I found his grave. All the dates and details match the ones on Mom's baptismal certificate, right down to his address."

"And your mom never knew him?" Both Pamela and Julie sang this out in unison. I admitted that something definitely seemed queer about the whole situation, but this all took place in the Roaring Twenties. Mom was born in 1922. Who could say what was happening back then?

"So let me get this straight. From what you're telling us, your grandfather was twenty-nine when your mother was born, and your grandmother was mid- forties." Julie swirled the ice around in her glass, staring down into it like one might do reading tea leaves.

"Yeah, she was forty-five. My mother called herself a 'change of life baby.'"

"And Grandma died when your mother was quite young, right?"

"Mom said she had a bad heart. A rheumatic heart, she called it. Mom was twelve when she lost her mother."

"And your mom was born at home," Julie continued.

"That's what she said. I'm pretty sure about that because there doesn't appear to be any hospital records of her birth. Her parents went down to the courthouse and applied for her birth certificate when she was a few days old."

"Your grandmother was forty-five and delivered a baby girl at home. In 1922. She had problems with her heart and died twelve years later," Julie reiterated matter-of-factly.

"Who raised your mother after Grandma died? She was only twelve," Pamela had scooted forward on the couch across from me and was staring at me with a strange "ah-ha" look.

"Her older half-sister, Charlotte," I replied. "My aunt."

"And Charlotte was how old when your mother was born?" Again, both girls asked the same question at the same time, although using different words. Through the jumbled sentences, the question was hard to decipher.

"Seventeen. My Aunt Charlotte was seventeen when my mother was born."

Julie and Pamela glanced at each other, then stared at me in disbelief. Not for the first time since I'd started back to school as one of the more "mature" students, I felt completely stupid. They were gawking at me as though I were an idiot.

"Don't you get it?" Julie's voice had elevated, so it was bouncing off the walls of the deserted common room. "Aunt Charlotte wasn't your aunt! She was your grandmother!"

Stories told to children by their parents tend to mark them, since a young mind absorbs information from that source as gospel. Memories such etched are so permanent that we grow up and go out into the world without questioning them, accepting them as absolute truth, as though the facts are indelibly carved.

My mother told me that Charlotte was my aunt. She always called her "Sis." I never thought to question what I accepted as absolute truth.

I wonder, even now, if Mom ever really knew the truth.

Could Charlotte have birthed that child, and not the forty-five-year old Minnie, whose delicate heart failed her just twelve years later? Could the seventeen-year- old Charlotte have been mother, and not older half-sister? Entirely possible. Undoubtedly, in those times, a sixteen-year-old getting pregnant by an older man would have been a scandal, a source of unspeakable family shame.

Stories told that "Aunt" Charlotte had a reputation as a "floozy". I love that word, and honestly thought it was one of my father's verbal fabrications until I saw the word in print in a book, ironically, that Aunt Charlotte gave me. A floozy means loose woman, which is how many thought of the flapper.

My brother confirmed the story we'd heard from those few distant cousins, one Charlotte herself shared with me when I was about sixteen. She described her days as a young woman living in Greenwich Village, working as a "Girl Friday" who became the mistress of a wealthy businessman. For her, this was no source of shame. In fact, she bragged about her good fortune. Her family was poor; but during those years in "the Village," she'd never lived better.

He bought me mink coats, wined and dined me, and took me shopping on Fifth Avenue. I had the best of everything. I had a hat to go with every outfit.

Might this lover have had a portrait done of his special lady, by some artist they passed on the streets of Greenwich Village?

I can picture Charlotte in the years before she moved to Greenwich Village, still living in now-defunct Winfield, at home with her mother Minnie. They were undoubtedly living lean. Her dad had disappeared from the picture, and her mother was working as a "washerwoman" to support herself, her two children, and an elderly mother.

I'm guessing Charlotte was a fractious teenager. All the glamour and excitement of the "new-age woman," the Flappers of the 1920s, was blossoming around her. She cared about her looks and she loved fashion, particularly hats. Is it possible that Charlotte caught the eye of a young man named Peter Fischer one night when she was only sixteen?

Grandpa was in his late twenties, just back from the service, and probably lonely. He lived just a few doors down.

***

A few months after Susie's wedding, she returned to Massachusetts for a visit. She appeared from within the crowd at Logan Airport, wearing a gray, denim carpenter's hat pulled down over her ears, her ponytail trailing out the back. She looked cute and casual in her faded jeans and thermal pullover. For one who never cared about being a girl, Susie always managed to look like she'd just stepped off a runway. Even when lugging a suitcase that was bigger than she was. After struggling with her just-barely-under-the-fifty-pound-limit luggage and hoisting it up onto the tailgate, we started the hour- long drive home.

I'm always curious about Susie's fashion opinion. I brought up the subject of the recent Royal Wedding of Prince William and Catherine Middleton.

"So, what'd you think anyway?" I asked. "Kate's dress was pretty, wasn't it?"

"Eh?" she shrugged. "She was pretty and all, but I can't believe she didn't even put up her hair. And that suit he had on—ugh. I'm glad Eddie didn't show up in crimson and gold." She wriggled her shoulders in disgust. "But, boy there were some hats in that crowd, weren't there?"

"I almost bought a hat to wear to your wedding," I said.

"Why didn't you, Mama?"

"I don't know. I guess I was afraid people would think I was trying to upstage the bride."

"It wouldn't have bothered me one bit. You should have worn a hat. You look so pretty in them. We both do."

It was true, I'd searched for a hat for Susie's wedding. At first, I shopped in the mall for something suitable, but hats for the purpose of pretty rather than practical seem to have gone out of style in this country. Macy's had a few, but my choices were limited, the contenders a purple felt fedora that screamed frumpy and a cotton candy pink, floppy-brimmed thing with more flowers on it than a table centerpiece.

So I went onto the Internet to see what the various bridal companies had to offer. Surely, a business as vast as David's Bridal would have hats to coordinate with their dresses. Since that's where my dress came from, I figured it was a good place to start. When the page came up for the search term hats, I was excited, then quickly disillusioned. A "vintage inspired" hat with veil came in white for the bride. I scrolled down and clicked on one of the only other two images. One was a baseball cap with the words "Mother of the Bride" spelled out in silver crystals above the brim. The other was a matching one labeled "Bride."

Google searches for "hat" produced websites with an amazing assortment of sizes and colors for men, women, and children. Unfortunately, every one was some variation of the baseball cap. I found only one or two shops specializing in fancy, big-brimmed hats, designed specifically for the Kentucky Derby.

Is it possible, I thought, that the only time it's acceptable to wear a hat in the United States anymore is to a Kentucky Derby party?

Not so in Great Britain. Hats are still very popular there and not just simple baseball or ski caps. Almost every female guest at the Royal Wedding flaunted a different design of hat, although some approached the bizarre. Princess Beatrice wore what the media described as a "cartoonish" oversized ribbon-shaped concoction that made it difficult for her to navigate, especially in and out of automobiles. But Beatrice had the last laugh. The hat sold at a charity auction several weeks after the wedding for more than $130,000.

Why has the custom of wearing hats seen such a decline on this side of the ocean over the last fifty-odd years? I began to feel a little sad, since back in the day, as my daughter would say, when my grandmother was a little girl, hats in the Big Apple were all the rage.

Vogue magazine tried. In early 2011, they printed a feature on hats and their possible resurrection in the fashion world of states-side couture. A photo study illustrated hats on the covers of their magazine from the 1930s forward. Unfortunately, it seems as though these decorative head dressings, much like the extreme clothing styles that parade down the runways at New York and Paris fashion shows, haven't often survived to the street level. At least, not yet.

My aunt Charlotte loved hats. I'd just turned thirteen when she gave me Lilly Dache's Glamour Book. It was at a time in my life when I was first daring to flap my own wings.

Dache began her career as an early 20th century hat designer. She stated, "For as you hitch your wagon to a star, so have I hitched my career to a hat." Beginning with her first turban, fashioned from scraps in a tiny, rented shop, Dache eventually built a skyscraper devoted to fashion and beauty on Madison Avenue. There were nine floors in all, one, of course, devoted exclusively to hats. The rest became, as Lilly said, "a vast laboratory of glamour."

In her second book, Talking Through My Hats, Dache wrote passionately of her devotion to her one and only husband. Although she flaunted her creativity and independence during working hours, the evenings and weekends "belong to my husband, Jean." It seems that although Lilly embraced the spirit of the times, she somehow maintained a happy balance between suffragette, entrepreneur, and loving wife—apparent contradictions to an ultimate degree.

Lilly Dache's story is one of Flapper Cinderella. Although I am sure she was uniquely talented, I contend that her success was also a case of incredibly apt timing. The conditions in metropolitan New York were just right in the 1920s and 30s for a woman to break out of the Victorian mold, in more ways than one. She wrote, "…a woman may buy a gay and daring hat as a gesture, to say to the world, 'See, I have not been beaten yet.'"

Charlotte's gift to me, the original 1956 edition, still sits on my bookshelf; its rose, linen cover faded almost to cream. I've read it cover to cover countless times. Often, I've referred to it as my Beauty Bible. But I never open the Dache book, touch its cover, or thumb through its delicate pages without thinking of my late aunt.

Charlotte was apparently a precocious young woman, probably typical of the fledgling suffragettes of 1920s New York. She styled her hair short, wore makeup and provocative clothes. She smoked, and she drank. As my mother always so delicately put it, she "liked her men." Daddy called her a floozy.

Charlotte bragged about the days she spent in Greenwich Village. She spoke freely of her days as a wealthy man's mistress; and how for a short time during her youth, she lived like a princess. That is how

Charlotte earned her fashion savvy. Her lover took her to all the expensive dress shops, on Broadway and Fifth Avenue, and bought her the best of everything.

"I always did have a sexy set of gams," she'd boast. "My man made sure I had plenty of skirts to show them off. And I had a hat to go with every outfit."

Perhaps, on one such shopping trip, this lover had a portrait done of his special lady, by some artist they passed on the streets of Greenwich Village. Perhaps that portrait now sits on the mantle in my office. Perhaps the portrait of my grandmother is also a portrait of Charlotte.

My memories of these stories are faded and fragmented. I was only a child when I heard them directly from Charlotte. She died when I was seventeen. My own mother, her "half-sister" or maybe even her daughter, never spoke of those times of Charlotte's life, at least not to me. She always seemed embarrassed when Charlotte herself began reminiscing.

Aunt Charlotte gave me Lilly Dache's Glamour Book, all about hats. She made me promise that when I was old enough to drive, I would take her shopping for hats. Sadly, that never happened.

Was she trying to tell me something without actually saying the words? Was she trying to feed me clues about her true identity, that perhaps the portrait of "my grandmother" wearing the cloche hat was really her?

Or was she only trying to prove to me, by showcasing Dache's story, that a woman didn't have to be a wallflower—meek and conservative—to maintain a successful marriage? By giving me that book, was Charlotte teaching me that it was possible to be an independent, attractive, sexual female and maintain a stable, happy marital union at the same time?

I know this; the woman known to me as my mother's half-sister was at the right age in the 1920s to embrace the spirit of the flappers.

If they'd ever met (and it's a secret thrill to think they could have), Charlotte would have been Lilly Dache's best friend. I can imagine them shopping together, excitedly trying on outfits, and choosing matching hats.

I still think about the woman I saw that day on the Boston Red Line, the one wearing the fur cloche. I wonder if the personality her hat shouted to the world spoke truth about her character. I wonder if it was the only way she spoke that truth, or if she lived it, up front, out in the open, in everything she did. I wonder if the woman on the subway will still color her hair, take care of her complexion, and wear bright red lipstick, even when she's old.

Charlotte did. I'll bet Susie will. I hope I do, too.

Woven Whole

In the words of Lilly Dache, a woman chooses a hat to make a statement: "This is who I am," or "This is who I would like to be." I believe Ms. Dache was right. I declare that credo holds whether the hat worn is a concrete article of clothing or an unseen symbolic presence.

We all wear hats that are invisible to the onlooker, at least at first glance. My mother wore a number of virtual hats, most triumphantly a Victorian bonnet signifying the perfect, purely innocent mother and wife. She undoubtedly earned that title and lived up to its rigors every day of her life. But underneath that façade, she wore a sheer black shroud, one that no one could see. Although I now think I understand why, it is sad to think she felt destined to wear that dark film of shame.

My daughter has already worn many hats in her life. She has been the precocious, little girl in the Easter bonnet, the tomboy in the baseball cap, and twice she's flaunted the proud, square hat of graduate. She's worn the feathers of a young girl dancing with her mommy in a dance pageant, and later, the less innocent plumes of a sassy young woman discovering her sexuality. She donned a tiara of crystals and pearls from which a bridal veil flowed. Today she wears the sensible, dignified hat of teacher. Her most recent addition has been the mommy hat, and she has embraced the role with enviable enthusiasm.

Susie is so much like Charlotte, who wore whatever the hell kind of hat she pleased.

I believe it was Charlotte who sported the cloche of the flapper in the portrait. I'll bet sometimes her hat was bright red and trimmed with tall feathers she was sure would draw attention. She wore a more conservative hat of working mother, but neither age nor circumstance tamped down the flapper. Her flamboyant spirit endured well into her senior years.

The hat Charlotte wore for me was that of caring aunt, but she was much more than just my aunt. In retrospect, I now see her devotion, her influence, as something more. Something, perhaps, more significant. It is frightening that the thread connecting generations is so tenuous, even within a single family. Without these pages I've written, my grandchildren would know even less about my mother's story than I do. They would know nothing about Charlotte. What a travesty. My mother and Charlotte might become strange faces in old photographs. I do not want them, or me, to become cardboard cutouts. My wish is that the names and the stories and the mysteries will be passed down.

I believe maternal threads continue to connect, even after the umbilical cord is broken.

The hard fact is that I will never be able to prove Charlotte was my grandmother. Except for in my heart. The role she played in my mother's life, and in mine, is part evidence. I believe if not in truth, then surely in essence, Charlotte earned the title of grandmother. She definitely wore that hat for me.

I believe it is Charlotte who watches me from my mantle as I write these words. I believe it is her spirit who persistently nudged me through an awkward, sometimes painful blossoming from the shy, overly protected, Catholic child into the way-more-confident woman I am today—the one who has and continues to strive for new horizons, no matter what her age.

But Charlotte went one step further. Though now only from my memory and the cold, impartial grave, she somehow brought me to clearer understanding of my mother. I no longer agonize over why Mom and I weren't closer. I no longer blame myself. I can comfortably acknowledge that we were simply very different women. Just like Susie and me. My daughter is the proof. I see in her a flapper; the spirit of a defiantly independent yet caring, compassionate woman with a true regard for family. Just like Charlotte.

What hat do I wear? I've come a ways from the plaid cap of Our Lady of Mt. Carmel. Over the decades, I've worn the hats of loving daughter, faithful wife, and doting mother. I've expressed my creativity wearing the hat of fashion designer, and now, as a writer. I continue to wear the hat of career woman, "the boss" from nine to five. And oh, how I cherish my newest hat, Grandma. Tentatively, a few times in my life, I've tried on the cloche of the flapper. Until now, I've never had the confidence to pull it off. Today, I believe I could. Creepy Harry be damned.

I've spent over fifty years searching for the hat that would complete me, fill out my half tree. What I've discovered is that sometimes you can't complete yourself by looking ahead, searching for an answer in some future accomplishment, some achievement, some skill you've yet to master. Sometimes you have to turn around, do a little painful digging into your roots, in order to find the key to what's missing in your life.

I was lucky. My key sprang up right in front of me with an in-your-face declaration. She is my daughter, a sneaky little genetic gift from Charlotte. Susie is a mirror of the past.

Ah, my Susie. Sometimes it seems as though she fell from a distant star. She is so much more than my daughter; she's my best friend. We live, physically, over 1200 miles apart. In personality, the distance approaches a light year. Yet the two of us couldn't possibly be closer. Exploring my maternal history, along with women's changing roles over the past millennium, has given me the courage to accept and treasure my daughter for who she is.

And, finally, myself. Now I feel whole.

******

About the Author

Frances Susanne Brown, writing under the pseudonym *Claire Gem*, has authored six novels and a writer's resource guide. The first in her "Haunted Voices" series, *Hearts Unloched*, won honors in the 2016 New York Book Festival, as well in the 2017 RONE Awards. Her other titles have been recognized by the American Fiction Awards, the HOLT Medallion Awards, and the National Reader's Choice Awards. Brown holds her MFA in creative writing from Lesley University, and currently works for Tufts University. She lives in Massachusetts with her husband. You can find out more at "Claire's" website:

www.clairegem.com

Made in the USA
Columbia, SC
12 September 2018